# THE RULE OF ST. BENEDICT
## IN ENGLISH

# THE RULE OF ST. BENEDICT
# IN ENGLISH

*Editor*
Timothy Fry, O.S.B.

*Associate Editors*
Imogene Baker, O.S.B.
Timothy Horner, O.S.B.
Augusta Raabe, O.S.B.
Mark Sheridan, O.S.B.

THE LITURGICAL PRESS
Collegeville, Minnesota
1982

For the scriptural passages quoted in this translation, the Vulgate numbering of chapters is followed; for the psalms, the Hebrew numbers are also given. Direct quotations from Scripture are italicized. The Latin text from which this translation was made is that of J. Neufville in A. de Vogüé, *La Règle de saint Benoît*, Sources Chrétiennes 181–182 (Paris: Les Éditions du Cerf 1972). The translation is taken from the unabridged edition of *RB 1980: The Rule of St. Benedict in Latin and English with Notes*, ed. Timothy Fry, O.S.B. (Collegeville, Minn.: The Liturgical Press 1981). Readers may refer to this unabridged edition for an account of the monks and nuns involved in the work of translation and for information on monastic subjects.

*Cover design by Ann Blattner.*

THE LITURGICAL PRESS
Collegeville, Minnesota 56321

# CONTENTS

# PREFACE

Pope John Paul II addressed two documents in 1981 to the entire Catholic Church and to "all men and women of good will." Inspired by a most urgent desire to help people improve their basic human relations, he wrote the encyclical "On Human Work" and the apostolic exhortation "The Role of the Family in Modern Society." St. Benedict's times were as turbulent as our own, though for very different reasons. He wrote his Rule primarily for monks, but its sound principles for working together and living together have proved relevant to people of all classes of society through fifteen hundred years.

Benedict (c. 480–547) lived in sixth-century Italy when the great Roman Empire was disintegrating. Rome had fallen to the barbarians in 410 and was sacked again in 455. Romulus Augustulus, the last emperor, was deposed in 476. Theodoric of the Ostrogoths maintained peace during a long reign (493–526), but upon his death the Eastern emperor Justinian tried to regain Rome, and through the remaining years of the century there was constant war as other barbarian tribes invaded the Italian peninsula.

Sometime during the reign of Theodoric, Benedict as a young man left his native Nursia in

Umbria to attend school in Rome, but became disgusted with the paganism he saw and renounced the world to live in solitude in a cave at Subiaco, some thirty miles east of Rome. Evidently he had undergone a deep religious experience. In time he came to the notice of people in the neighborhood, and some monks asked him to be their abbot. He consented with reluctance, and after some time the recalcitrant monks sought to poison him. Later another group of monks joined him, and he established twelve monasteries of twelve monks each.

Experience with the envy of the local clergy led Benedict to abandon this settlement, and with some disciples he founded a monastery on the mountain above Cassino, about eighty miles south of Rome. His fame as a holy person spread throughout the area; even the king of the Goths, Totila, came to see him. About the year 547 he died. Pope St. Gregory the Great (590–604), whose second book of *The Dialogues* is the only source for information on St. Benedict, notes that St. Scholastica was his sister (traditionally known as his twin sister).

Apart from these meager facts, nothing more is known of the life of St. Benedict. But most of the information from St. Gregory can be corroborated by other historical events of the time. Gregory did not set out to write a biography; his purpose was to show that there were holy people in Italy, not just in the East, and that St. Benedict was a great miracle-worker. He mentions the Rule of

St. Benedict and commends it for its discretion and lucidity of style. "If anyone wishes to know his character and life more precisely, he may find in the ordinances of that Rule a complete account of the abbot's practice; for the holy man cannot have taught otherwise than as he lived."

Writers after St. Gregory have noted the same discretion in St. Benedict's Rule, and this quality more than any other accounts in great part for its longevity. The fact that many men and women throughout the world live it today is supporting evidence.

In the unsettled, strife-torn Italy of the sixth century, Benedict's Rule offered definitive direction and established an ordered way of life that gave security and stability. He sought to lay down "nothing harsh, nothing burdensome," but was intent on encouraging the person coming to the monastery: "Do not be daunted immediately by fear and run away from the road that leads to salvation."

Benedict calls his Rule "a little rule for beginners." It contains directions for all aspects of the monastic life, from establishing the abbot as superior, the arrangement of psalms for prayers, measures for correction of faults, to details of clothing and the amount of food and drink. The reader will note that some customs are outmoded today, and monks have accordingly modified some of these.

St. Benedict taught that if the monk seeks to answer the call of God — "If you hear his voice today, do not harden your heart" — then he must put all else aside and follow the teaching of Christ in obedience. To this end St. Benedict established a "school for the Lord's service," a place where monks learn to serve the Lord in obedience to their abbot, who "is believed to hold the place of Christ." His spirituality is Christocentric: "the love of Christ must come before all else." After a year of trial, the novice promises stability, fidelity to monastic life, and obedience. St. Benedict expected his monks to advance on the "path of God's commandments, [their] hearts overflowing with the inexpressible delight of love."

Benedict was a keen observer of human nature and realized that people often fail (the abbot must "distrust his own frailty"). He was concerned to help the weak, and consequently he enjoined that the abbot "so regulate and arrange all matters that souls may be saved and the brothers may go about their activities without justifiable grumbling." Benedict looked to the heart; he sought a spirit of willingness ("First and foremost, there must be no word or sign of the evil of grumbling, no manifestation of it for any reason at all") and sincerity ("Never give a hollow greeting of peace"; "Let us stand to sing the psalms in such a way that our minds are in harmony with our voices").

The so-called penal code (chs. 23–30, 43–46) is more accurately seen as correctional measures designed for the reformation and healing of the person, not a rigid, brutal structure imposed legalistically. St. Benedict stressed the importance of the person and the relationship of persons living together. He respected the freedom of the person (the novice is free to leave at any time; the monk who leaves may be received back even a third time). If there is strictness, the purpose is to "amend faults and safeguard love." He directed the abbot to "arrange everything that the strong have something to yearn for and the weak nothing to run from." It is a humane approach to personal relationships. But it is an approach based on the supernatural: "that in all things God may be glorified." Benedict was a God-oriented man leading like-minded people on the way of the Gospel. In St. Gregory's words, he was a man of God (*vir Dei*).

REV. TIMOTHY FRY, O.S.B.

St. Benedict's Abbey
Atchison, Kansas

*Feast of St. Benedict*
*21 March 1982*

# THE RULE OF SAINT BENEDICT

¹Listen carefully, my son, to the master's instructions, and attend to them with the ear of your heart. This is advice from a father who loves you; welcome it, and faithfully put it into practice. ²The labor of obedience will bring you back to him from whom you had drifted through the sloth of disobedience. ³This message of mine is for you, then, if you are ready to give up your own will, once and for all, and armed with the strong and noble weapons of obedience to do battle for the true King, Christ the Lord.

⁴First of all, every time you begin a good work, you must pray to him most earnestly to bring it to perfection. ⁵In his goodness, he has already counted us as his sons, and therefore we should never grieve him by our evil actions. ⁶With his good gifts which are in us, we must obey him at all times that he may never become the angry father who disinherits his sons, ⁷nor the dread lord, enraged by our sins, who punishes us forever as worthless servants for refusing to follow him to glory.

⁸Let us get up then, at long last, for the Scriptures rouse us when they say: *It is high time for us to arise from sleep* (Rom 13:11). ⁹Let us open

our eyes to the light that comes from God, and our ears to the voice from heaven that every day calls out this charge: [10]*If you hear his voice today, do not harden your hearts* (Ps 94 [95]:8). [11]And again: *You that have ears to hear, listen to what the Spirit says to the churches* (Rev 2:7). [12]And what does he say? *Come and listen to me, sons; I will teach you the fear of the Lord* (Ps 33[34]:12). [13]*Run while you have the light* of life, *that the darkness* of death *may not overtake you* (John 12:35).

[14]Seeking his workman in a multitude of people, the Lord calls out to him and lifts his voice again: [15]*Is there anyone here who yearns for life and desires to see good days?* (Ps 33[34]:13) [16]If you hear this and your answer is "I do," God then directs these words to you: [17]If you desire true and eternal life, *keep your tongue free from vicious talk and your lips from all deceit; turn away from evil and do good; let peace be your quest and aim* (Ps 33[34]:14-15). [18]Once you have done this, my *eyes will be upon* you *and* my *ears will listen* for your *prayers; and even before you ask me, I will say* to you: *Here I am* (Isa 58:9). [19]What, dear brothers, is more delightful than this voice of the Lord calling to us? [20]See how the Lord in his love shows us the way of life. [21]Clothed then with faith and the performance of good works, let us set out on this way, with the Gospel for our guide, that we may deserve to see him *who has called* us *to his kingdom* (1 Thess 2:12).

²²If we wish to dwell in the tent of this kingdom, we will never arrive unless we run there by doing good deeds. ²³But let us ask the Lord with the Prophet: *Who will dwell in your tent, Lord; who will find rest upon your holy mountain?* (Ps 14[15]:1) ²⁴After this question, brothers, let us listen well to what the Lord says in reply, for he shows us the way to his tent. ²⁵*One who walks without blemish*, he says, *and is just in all his dealings*; ²⁶*who speaks the truth from his heart and has not practiced deceit with his tongue*; ²⁷*who has not wronged a fellowman in any way, nor listened to slanders against his neighbor* (Ps 14[15]:2-3). ²⁸He has *foiled* the *evil one*, the devil, at every turn, flinging both him and his promptings far *from the sight* of his heart. While these temptations were still *young, he caught hold of them and dashed them against* Christ (Ps 14[15]:4; 136[137]:9). ²⁹These people *fear the Lord*, and do not become elated over their good deeds; they judge it is the Lord's power, not their own, that brings about the good in them. ³⁰*They praise* (Ps 14[15]:4) the Lord working in them, and say with the Prophet: *Not to us, Lord, not to us give the glory, but to your name alone* (Ps 113[115:1]:9). ³¹In just this way Paul the Apostle refused to take credit for the power of his preaching. He declared: *By God's grace I am what I am* (1 Cor 15:10). ³²And again he said: *He who boasts should make his boast in the Lord* (2 Cor 10:17). ³³That is why the Lord says in the Gospel: *Whoever hears these words of mine and does*

*them is like a wise man who built his house upon rock;* [34]*the floods came and the winds blew and beat against the house, but it did not fall: it was founded on rock* (Matt 7:24-25).

[35]With this conclusion, the Lord waits for us daily to translate into action, as we should, his holy teachings. [36]Therefore our life span has been lengthened by way of a truce, that we may amend our misdeeds. [37]As the Apostle says: *Do you not know that the patience of God is leading you to repent* (Rom 2:4)? [38]And indeed the Lord assures us in his love: *I do not wish the death of the sinner, but that he turn back to me and live* (Ezek 33:11).

[39]Brothers, now that we have asked the Lord who will dwell in his tent, we have heard the instruction for dwelling in it, but only if we fulfill the obligations of those who live there. [40]We must, then, prepare our hearts and bodies for the battle of holy obedience to his instructions. [41]What is not possible to us by nature, let us ask the Lord to supply by the help of his grace. [42]If we wish to reach eternal life, even as we avoid the torments of hell, [43]then — while there is still time, while we are in this body and have time to accomplish all these things by the light of life — [44]we must run and do now what will profit us forever.

[45]Therefore we intend to establish a school for the Lord's service. [46]In drawing up its regulations, we hope to set down nothing harsh, nothing burdensome. [47]The good of all concerned,

however, may prompt us to a little strictness in order to amend faults and to safeguard love. [48]Do not be daunted immediately by fear and run away from the road that leads to salvation. It is bound to be narrow at the outset. [49]But as we progress in this way of life and in faith, we shall run on the path of God's commandments, our hearts overflowing with the inexpressible delight of love. [50]Never swerving from his instructions, then, but faithfully observing his teaching in the monastery until death, we shall through patience share in the sufferings of Christ that we may deserve also to share in his kingdom. Amen.

[It is called a rule because it regulates
the lives of those who obey it]

## CHAPTER 1. THE KINDS OF MONKS

¹There are clearly four kinds of monks. ²First, there are the cenobites, that is to say, those who belong to a monastery, where they serve under a rule and an abbot.

³Second, there are the anchorites or hermits, who have come through the test of living in a monastery for a long time, and have passed beyond the first fervor of monastic life. ⁴Thanks to the help and guidance of many, they are now trained to fight against the devil. ⁵They have built up their strength and go from the battle line in the ranks of their brothers to the single combat of the desert. Self-reliant now, without the support of another, they are ready with God's help to grapple single-handed with the vices of body and mind.

⁶Third, there are the sarabaites, the most detestable kind of monks, who with no experience to guide them, no rule to try them *as gold is tried in a furnace* (Prov 27:21), have a character as soft as lead. ⁷Still loyal to the world by their actions, they clearly lie to God by their tonsure. ⁸Two or three together, or even alone, without a shepherd, they pen themselves up in their own sheepfolds, not the Lord's. Their law is what they

20

like to do, whatever strikes their fancy. ⁹Anything they believe in and choose, they call holy; anything they dislike, they consider forbidden.

¹⁰Fourth and finally, there are the monks called gyrovagues, who spend their entire lives drifting from region to region, staying as guests for three or four days in different monasteries. ¹¹Always on the move, they never settle down, and are slaves to their own wills and gross appetites. In every way they are worse than sarabaites.

¹²It is better to keep silent than to speak of all these and their disgraceful way of life. ¹³Let us pass them by, then, and with the help of the Lord, proceed to draw up a plan for the strong kind, the cenobites.

CHAPTER 2. QUALITIES OF THE ABBOT

¹To be worthy of the task of governing a monastery, the abbot must always remember what his title signifies and act as a superior should. ²He is believed to hold the place of Christ in the monastery, since he is addressed by a title of Christ, ³as the Apostle indicates: *You have received the spirit of adoption of sons by which we exclaim, abba, father* (Rom 8:15). ⁴Therefore, the abbot must never teach or decree or command anything that would deviate from the Lord's instructions. ⁵On the contrary, everything he teaches and commands should, like the leaven of divine justice, permeate the minds of his disciples. ⁶Let the abbot always remember that at the fearful judg-

ment of God, not only his teaching but also his
disciples' obedience will come under scrutiny.
⁷The abbot must, therefore, be aware that the
shepherd will bear the blame wherever the
father of the household finds that the sheep have
yielded no profit. ⁸Still, if he has faithfully
shepherded a restive and disobedient flock, always striving to cure their unhealthy ways, it will
be otherwise: ⁹the shepherd will be acquitted at
the Lord's judgment. Then, like the Prophet, he
may say to the Lord: *I have not hidden your justice in my heart; I have proclaimed your truth
and your salvation* (Ps 39[40]:11), *but they
spurned and rejected me* (Isa 1:2; Ezek 20:27).
¹⁰Then at last the sheep that have rebelled
against his care will be punished by the overwhelming power of death.

¹¹Furthermore, anyone who receives the name
of abbot is to lead his disciples by a twofold
teaching: ¹²he must point out to them all that is
good and holy more by example than by words,
proposing the commandments of the Lord to re-
ceptive disciples with words, but demonstrating
God's instructions to the stubborn and the dull by
a living example. ¹³Again, if he teaches his disciples that something is not to be done, then
neither must he do it, *lest after preaching to
others, he himself be found reprobate* (1 Cor
9:27) ¹⁴and God some day call to him in his sin:
*How is it that you repeat my just commands and
mouth my covenant when you hate discipline
and toss my words behind you* (Ps 49[50]:16-17)?

¹⁵And also this: *How is it that you can see a splinter in your brother's eye, and never notice the plank in your own* (Matt 7:3)?

¹⁶The abbot should avoid all favoritism in the monastery. ¹⁷He is not to love one more than another unless he finds someone better in good actions and obedience. ¹⁸A man born free is not to be given higher rank than a slave who becomes a monk, except for some other good reason. ¹⁹But the abbot is free, if he sees fit, to change anyone's rank as justice demands. Ordinarily, everyone is to keep to his regular place, ²⁰because *whether slave or free, we are all one in Christ* (Gal 3:28; Eph 6:8) and share alike in bearing arms in the service of the one Lord, for *God shows no partiality among persons* (Rom 2:11). ²¹Only in this are we distinguished in his sight: if we are found better than others in good works and in humility. ²²Therefore, the abbot is to show equal love to everyone and apply the same discipline to all according to their merits.

²³In his teaching, the abbot should always observe the Apostle's recommendation, in which he says: *Use argument, appeal, reproof* (2 Tim 4:2). ²⁴This means that he must vary with circumstances, threatening and coaxing by turns, stern as a taskmaster, devoted and tender as only a father can be. ²⁵With the undisciplined and restless, he will use firm argument; with the obedient and docile and patient, he will appeal for greater virtue; but as for the negligent and disdainful, we charge him to use reproof and re-

buke. [26]He should not gloss over the sins of those
who err, but cut them out while he can, as soon as
they begin to sprout, remembering the fate of Eli,
priest of Shiloh (1 Sam 2:11–4:18). [27]For upright
and perceptive men, his first and second warnings should be verbal; [28]but those who are evil or
stubborn, arrogant or disobedient, he can curb
only by blows or some other physical punishment at the first offense. It is written, *The fool
cannot be corrected with words* (Prov 29:19);
[29]and again, *Strike your son with a rod and you
will free his soul from death* (Prov 23:14).

[30]The abbot must always remember what he is
and remember what he is called, aware that more
will be expected of a man to whom more has
been entrusted. [31]He must know what a difficult
and demanding burden he has undertaken: di-
recting souls and serving a variety of tempera-
ments, coaxing, reproving and encouraging them
as appropriate. [32]He must so accommodate and
adapt himself to each one's character and intelli-
gence that he will not only keep the flock entrusted to his care from dwindling, but will re-
joice in the increase of a good flock. [33]Above all,
he must not show too great concern for the fleet-
ing and temporal things of this world, neglecting
or treating lightly the welfare of those entrusted
to him. [34]Rather, he should keep in mind that he
has undertaken the care of souls for whom he
must give an account. [35]That he may not plead
lack of resources as an excuse, he is to remember
what is written: *Seek first the kingdom of God*

*and his justice, and all these things will be given you as well* (Matt 6:33), <sup>36</sup>and again, *Those who fear him lack nothing* (Ps 33[34]:10).

<sup>37</sup>The abbot must know that anyone undertaking the charge of souls must be ready to account for them. <sup>38</sup>Whatever the number of brothers he has in his care, let him realize that on judgment day he will surely have to submit a reckoning to the Lord for all their souls — and indeed for his own as well. <sup>39</sup>In this way, while always fearful of the future examination of the shepherd about the sheep entrusted to him and careful about the state of others' accounts, he becomes concerned also about his own, <sup>40</sup> and while helping others to amend by his warnings, he achieves the amendment of his own faults.

### CHAPTER 3. SUMMONING THE BROTHERS FOR COUNSEL

<sup>1</sup>As often as anything important is to be done in the monastery, the abbot shall call the whole community together and himself explain what the business is; <sup>2</sup>and after hearing the advice of the brothers, let him ponder it and follow what he judges the wiser course. <sup>3</sup>The reason why we have said all should be called for counsel is that the Lord often reveals what is better to the younger. <sup>4</sup>The brothers, for their part, are to express their opinions with all humility, and not presume to defend their own views obstinately. <sup>5</sup>The decision is rather the abbot's to make, so

that when he has determined what is more prudent, all may obey. ⁶Nevertheless, just as it is proper for disciples to obey their master, so it is becoming for the master on his part to settle everything with foresight and fairness.

⁷Accordingly in every instance, all are to follow the teaching of the rule, and no one shall rashly deviate from it. ⁸In the monastery no one is to follow his own heart's desire, ⁹nor shall anyone presume to contend with his abbot defiantly, or outside the monastery. ¹⁰Should anyone presume to do so, let him be subjected to the discipline of the rule. ¹¹Moreover, the abbot himself must fear God and keep the rule in everything he does; he can be sure beyond any doubt that he will have to give an account of all his judgments to God, the most just of judges.

¹²If less important business of the monastery is to be transacted, he shall take counsel with the seniors only, ¹³as it is written: *Do everything with counsel and you will not be sorry afterward* (Sir 32:24).

CHAPTER 4. THE TOOLS FOR GOOD WORKS

¹First of all, *love the Lord God with your whole heart, your whole soul and all your strength*, ²*and love your neighbor as yourself* (Matt 22:37-39; Mark 12:30-31; Luke 10:27). ³Then the following: *You are not to kill*, ⁴*not to commit adultery*; ⁵*you are not to steal* ⁶*nor to covet* (Rom 13:9); ⁷*you are not to bear false wit-*

*ness* (Matt 19:18; Mark 10:19; Luke 18:20). [8]*You must honor everyone* (1 Pet 2:17), [9]and *never do to another what you do not want done to yourself* (Tob 4:16; Matt 7:12; Luke 6:31).

[10]*Renounce yourself in order to follow Christ* (Matt 16:24; Luke 9:23); [11]*discipline your body* (1 Cor 9:27); [12]do not pamper yourself, [13]but love fasting. [14]You must relieve the lot of the poor, [15]*clothe the naked,* [16]*visit the sick* (Matt 25:36), [17]and bury the dead. [18]Go to help the troubled [19]and console the sorrowing.

[20]Your way of acting should be different from the world's way; [21]the love of Christ must come before all else. [22]You are not to act in anger [23]or nurse a grudge. [24]Rid your heart of all deceit. [25]Never give a hollow greeting of peace [26]or turn away when someone needs your love. [27]Bind yourself to no oath lest it prove false, [28]but speak the truth with heart and tongue.

[29]*Do not repay one bad turn with another* (1 Thess 5:15; 1 Pet 3:9). [30]Do not injure anyone, but bear injuries patiently. [31]*Love your enemies* (Matt 5:44; Luke 6:27). [32]If people curse you, do not curse them back but bless them instead. [33]*Endure persecution for the sake of justice* (Matt 5:10).

[34]You must *not* be *proud,* [35]*nor be given to wine* (Titus 1:7; 1 Tim 3:3). [36]Refrain from too much eating [37]or sleeping, [38]and *from laziness* (Rom 12:11). [39]Do not grumble [40]or speak ill of others.

[41]Place your hope in God alone. [42]If you notice

something good in yourself, give credit to God, not to yourself, ⁴³but be certain that the evil you commit is always your own and yours to acknowledge.

⁴⁴Live in fear of judgment day ⁴⁵and have a great horror of hell. ⁴⁶Yearn for everlasting life with holy desire. ⁴⁷Day by day remind yourself that you are going to die. ⁴⁸Hour by hour keep careful watch over all you do, ⁴⁹aware that God's gaze is upon you, wherever you may be. ⁵⁰As soon as wrongful thoughts come into your heart, dash them against Christ and disclose them to your spiritual father. ⁵¹Guard your lips from harmful or deceptive speech. ⁵²Prefer moderation in speech ⁵³and speak no foolish chatter, nothing just to provoke laughter; ⁵⁴do not love immoderate or boisterous laughter.

⁵⁵Listen readily to holy reading, ⁵⁶and devote yourself often to prayer. ⁵⁷Every day with tears and sighs confess your past sins to God in prayer ⁵⁸and change from these evil ways in the future.

⁵⁹*Do not gratify the promptings of the flesh* (Gal 5:16); ⁶⁰hate the urgings of self-will. ⁶¹Obey the orders of the abbot unreservedly, even if his own conduct—which God forbid—be at odds with what he says. Remember the teaching of the Lord: *Do what they say, not what they do* (Matt 23:3).

⁶²Do not aspire to be called holy before you really are, but first be holy that you may more truly be called so. ⁶³Live by God's commandments every day; ⁶⁴treasure chastity, ⁶⁵har-

bor neither hatred ⁶⁶nor jealousy of anyone, ⁶⁷and do nothing out of envy. ⁶⁸Do not love quarreling; ⁶⁹shun arrogance. ⁷⁰Respect the elders ⁷¹and love the young. ⁷²Pray for your enemies out of love for Christ. ⁷³If you have a dispute with someone, make peace with him before the sun goes down.

⁷⁴And finally, never lose hope in God's mercy.

⁷⁵These, then, are the tools of the spiritual craft. ⁷⁶When we have used them without ceasing day and night and have returned them on judgment day, our wages will be the reward the Lord has promised: ⁷⁷*What the eye has not seen nor the ear heard, God has prepared for those who love him* (1 Cor 2:9).

⁷⁸The workshop where we are to toil faithfully at all these tasks is the enclosure of the monastery and stability in the community.


CHAPTER 5. OBEDIENCE

¹The first step of humility is unhesitating obedience, ²which comes naturally to those who cherish Christ above all. ³Because of the holy service they have professed, or because of dread of hell and for the glory of everlasting life, ⁴they carry out the superior's order as promptly as if the command came from God himself. ⁵The Lord says of men like this: *No sooner did he hear than he obeyed me* (Ps 17[18]:45); ⁶again, he tells teachers: *Whoever listens to you, listens to me* (Luke 10:16). ⁷Such people as these immediately put aside their own concerns, abandon their own

will, ⁸and lay down whatever they have in hand, leaving it unfinished. With the ready step of obedience, they follow the voice of authority in their actions. ⁹Almost at the same moment, then, as the master gives the instruction the disciple quickly puts it into practice in the fear of God; and both actions together are swiftly completed as one.

¹⁰It is love that impels them to pursue everlasting life; ¹¹therefore, they are eager to take the narrow road of which the Lord says: *Narrow is the road that leads to life* (Matt 7:14). ¹²They no longer live by their own judgment, giving in to their whims and appetites; rather they walk according to another's decisions and directions, choosing to live in monasteries and to have an abbot over them. ¹³Men of this resolve unquestionably conform to the saying of the Lord: *I have come not to do my own will, but the will of him who sent me* (John 6:38).

¹⁴This very obedience, however, will be acceptable to God and agreeable to men only if compliance with what is commanded is not cringing or sluggish or half-hearted, but free from any grumbling or any reaction of unwillingness. ¹⁵For the obedience shown to superiors is given to God, as he himself said: *Whoever listens to you, listens to me* (Luke 10:16). ¹⁶Furthermore, the disciples' obedience must be given gladly, for *God loves a cheerful giver* (2 Cor 9:7). ¹⁷If a disciple obeys grudgingly and grumbles, not only aloud but also in his heart, ¹⁸then, even though

he carries out the order, his action will not be accepted with favor by God, who sees that he is grumbling in his heart. ¹⁹He will have no reward for service of this kind; on the contrary, he will incur punishment for grumbling, unless he changes for the better and makes amends.

### CHAPTER 6. RESTRAINT OF SPEECH

¹Let us follow the Prophet's counsel: *I said, I have resolved to keep watch over my ways that I may never sin with my tongue. I was silent and was humbled, and I refrained even from good words* (Ps 38[39]:2-3). ²Here the Prophet indicates that there are times when good words are to be left unsaid out of esteem for silence. For all the more reason, then, should evil speech be curbed so that punishment for sin may be avoided. ³Indeed, so important is silence that permission to speak should seldom be granted even to mature disciples, no matter how good or holy or constructive their talk, ⁴because it is written: *In a flood of words you will not avoid sin* (Prov 10:19); ⁵and elsewhere, *The tongue holds the key to life and death* (Prov 18:21). ⁶Speaking and teaching are the master's task; the disciple is to be silent and listen.

⁷Therefore, any requests to a superior should be made with all humility and respectful submission. ⁸We absolutely condemn in all places any vulgarity and gossip and talk leading to laughter, and we do not permit a disciple to engage in words of that kind.

### CHAPTER 7. HUMILITY

[1]Brothers, divine Scripture calls to us saying: *Whoever exalts himself shall be humbled, and whoever humbles himself shall be exalted* (Luke 14:11; 18:14). [2]In saying this, therefore, it shows us that every exaltation is a kind of pride, [3]which the Prophet indicates he has shunned, saying: *Lord, my heart is not exalted; my eyes are not lifted up and I have not walked in the ways of the great nor gone after marvels beyond me* (Ps 130[131]:1). [4]And why? *If I had not a humble spirit, but were exalted instead, then you would treat me like a weaned child on its mother's lap* (Ps 130[131]:2).

[5]Accordingly, brothers, if we want to reach the highest summit of humility, if we desire to attain speedily that exaltation in heaven to which we climb by the humility of this present life, [6]then by our ascending actions we must set up that ladder on which Jacob in a dream saw *angels descending and ascending* (Gen 28:12). [7]Without doubt, this descent and ascent can signify only that we descend by exaltation and ascend by humility. [8]Now the ladder erected is our life on earth, and if we humble our hearts the Lord will raise it to heaven. [9]We may call our body and soul the sides of this ladder, into which our divine vocation has fitted the various steps of humility and discipline as we ascend.

[10]The first step of humility, then, is that a man keeps the *fear of God* always *before his eyes* (Ps

35[36]:2) and never forgets it. ¹¹He must constantly remember everything God has commanded, keeping in mind that all who despise God will burn in hell for their sins, and all who fear God have everlasting life awaiting them. ¹²While he guards himself at every moment from sins and vices of thought or tongue, of hand or foot, of self-will or bodily desire, ¹³let him recall that he is always seen by God in heaven, that his actions everywhere are in God's sight and are reported by angels at every hour.

¹⁴The Prophet indicates this to us when he shows that our thoughts are always present to God, saying: *God searches hearts and minds* (Ps 7:10); ¹⁵again he says: *The Lord knows the thoughts of men* (Ps 93[94]:11); ¹⁶likewise, *From afar you know my thoughts* (Ps 138[139]:3); ¹⁷and, *The thought of man shall give you praise* (Ps 75[76]:11). ¹⁸That he may take care to avoid sinful thoughts, the virtuous brother must always say to himself: *I shall be blameless in his sight* if *I guard myself from my own wickedness* (Ps 17[18]:24).

¹⁹Truly, we are forbidden to do our own will, for Scripture tells us: *Turn away from your desires* (Sir 18:30). ²⁰And in the Prayer too we ask God that his *will be done* in us (Matt 6:10). ²¹We are rightly taught not to do our own will, since we dread what Scripture says: *There are ways which men call right that in the end plunge into the depths of hell* (Prov 16:25). ²²Moreover, we fear what is said of those who ignore this: *They are*

*corrupt and have become depraved in their de-
sires* (Ps 13[14]:1).

²³As for the desires of the body, we must believe that God is always with us, for *All my desires are known to you* (Ps 37[38]:10), as the
Prophet tells the Lord. ²⁴We must then be on
guard against any base desire, because death is
stationed near the gateway of pleasure. ²⁵For this
reason Scripture warns us, *Pursue not your lusts*
(Sir 18:30).

²⁶Accordingly, if *the eyes of the Lord are
watching the good and the wicked* (Prov 15:3),
²⁷if at all times *the Lord looks down from heaven
on the sons of men to see whether any understand and seek God* (Ps 13[14]:2); ²⁸and if
every day the angels assigned to us report our
deeds to the Lord day and night, ²⁹then, brothers,
we must be vigilant every hour or, as the Prophet
says in the psalm, God may observe us *falling* at
some time into evil and *so made worthless* (Ps
13[14]:3). ³⁰After sparing us for a while because
he is a loving father who waits for us to improve,
he may tell us later, *This you did, and I said
nothing* (Ps 49[50]:21).

³¹The second step of humility is that a man
loves not his own will nor takes pleasure in the
satisfaction of his desires; ³²rather he shall imitate by his actions that saying of the Lord: *I have
come not to do my own will, but the will of him
who sent me* (John 6:38). ³³Similarly we read,
"Consent merits punishment; constraint wins a
crown."

³⁴The third step of humility is that a man submits to his superior in all obedience for the love of God, imitating the Lord of whom the Apostle says: *He became obedient even to death* (Phil 2:8).

³⁵The fourth step of humility is that in this obedience under difficult, unfavorable, or even unjust conditions, his heart quietly embraces suffering ³⁶and endures it without weakening or seeking escape. For Scripture has it: *Anyone who perseveres to the end will be saved* (Matt 10:22), ³⁷and again, *Be brave of heart and rely on the Lord* (Ps 26[27]:14). ³⁸Another passage shows how the faithful must endure everything, even contradiction, for the Lord's sake, saying in the person of those who suffer, *For your sake we are put to death continually; we are regarded as sheep marked for slaughter* (Rom 8:36; Ps 43[44]:22). ³⁹They are so confident in their expectation of reward from God that they continue joyfully and say, *But in all this we overcome because of him who so greatly loved us* (Rom 8:37). ⁴⁰Elsewhere Scripture says: *O God, you have tested us, you have tried us as silver is tried by fire; you have led us into a snare, you have placed afflictions on our backs* (Ps 65[66]:10-11). ⁴¹Then, to show that we ought to be under a superior, it adds: *You have placed men over our heads* (Ps 65[66]:12).

⁴²In truth, those who are patient amid hardships and unjust treatment are fulfilling the Lord's command: *When struck on one cheek,*

*they turn the other; when deprived of their coat, they offer their cloak also; when pressed into service for one mile, they go two* (Matt 5:39-41). [43]With the Apostle Paul, they bear with *false brothers, endure persecution,* and *bless those who curse them* (2 Cor 11:26; 1 Cor 4:12).

[44]The fifth step of humility is that a man does not conceal from his abbot any sinful thoughts entering his heart, or any wrongs committed in secret, but rather confesses them humbly. [45]Concerning this, Scripture exhorts us: *Make known your way to the Lord and hope in him* (Ps 36[37]:5). [46]And again, *Confess to the Lord, for he is good; his mercy is forever* (Ps 105[106]:1; Ps 117[118]:1). [47]So too the Prophet: *To you I have acknowledged my offense; my faults I have not concealed.* [48]*I have said: Against myself I will report my faults to the Lord, and you have forgiven the wickedness of my heart* (Ps 31[32]:5).

[49]The sixth step of humility is that a monk is content with the lowest and most menial treatment, and regards himself as a poor and worthless workman in whatever task he is given, [50]saying to himself with the Prophet: *I am insignificant and ignorant, no better than a beast before you, yet I am with you always* (Ps 72[73]:22-23).

[51]The seventh step of humility is that a man not only admits with his tongue but is also convinced in his heart that he is inferior to all and of less value, [52]humbling himself and saying with the

Prophet: *I am truly a worm, not a man, scorned by men and despised by the people* (Ps 21[22]:7). ⁵³*I was exalted, then I was humbled and overwhelmed with confusion* (Ps 87[88]:16). ⁵⁴And again, *It is a blessing that you have humbled me so that I can learn your commandments* (Ps 118[119]:71,73).

⁵⁵The eighth step of humility is that a monk does only what is endorsed by the common rule of the monastery and the example set by his superiors.

⁵⁶The ninth step of humility is that a monk controls his tongue and remains silent, not speaking unless asked a question, ⁵⁷for Scripture warns, *In a flood of words you will not avoid sinning* (Prov 10:19), ⁵⁸and, *A talkative man goes about aimlessly on earth* (Ps 139[140]:12).

⁵⁹The tenth step of humility is that he is not given to ready laughter, for it is written: *Only a fool raises his voice in laughter* (Sir 21:23).

⁶⁰The eleventh step of humility is that a monk speaks gently and without laughter, seriously and with becoming modesty, briefly and reasonably, but without raising his voice, ⁶¹as it is written: "A wise man is known by his few words."

⁶²The twelfth step of humility is that a monk always manifests humility in his bearing no less than in his heart, so that it is evident ⁶³at the Work of God, in the oratory, the monastery or the garden, on a journey or in the field, or anywhere else. Whether he sits, walks or stands, his head must be bowed and his eyes cast down. ⁶⁴Judging

himself always guilty on account of his sins, he
should consider that he is already at the fearful
judgment, 65and constantly say in his heart what
the publican in the Gospel said with downcast
eyes: *Lord, I am a sinner, not worthy to look
up to heaven* (Luke 18:13). 66And with the
Prophet: *I am bowed down and humbled in
every way* (Ps 37[38]:7-9; Ps 118[119]:107).

67Now, therefore, after ascending all these
steps of humility, the monk will quickly arrive at
that *perfect love* of God which *casts out fear* (1
John 4:18). 68Through this love, all that he once
performed with dread, he will now begin to observe without effort, as though naturally, from
habit, 69no longer out of fear of hell, but out of
love for Christ, good habit and delight in virtue.
70All this the Lord will by the Holy Spirit gra-
ciously manifest in his workman now cleansed of
vices and sins.


CHAPTER 8.  THE DIVINE OFFICE AT NIGHT

1During the winter season, that is, from the first
of November until Easter, it seems reasonable to
arise at the eighth hour of the night. 2By sleeping
until a little past the middle of the night, the
brothers can arise with their food fully digested.
3In the time remaining after Vigils, those who
need to learn some of the psalter or readings
should study them.

4Between Easter and the first of November
mentioned above, the time for Vigils should be

adjusted so that a very short interval after Vigils will give the monks opportunity to care for nature's needs. Then, at daybreak, Lauds should follow immediately.

## CHAPTER 9. THE NUMBER OF PSALMS AT THE NIGHT OFFICE

[1]During the winter season, Vigils begin with the verse: *Lord, open my lips and my mouth shall proclaim your praise* (Ps 50[51]:17). After this has been said three times, [2]the following order is observed: Psalm 3 with "Glory be to the Father"; [3]Psalm 94 with a refrain, or at least chanted; [4]an Ambrosian hymn; then six psalms with refrain.

[5]After the psalmody, a versicle is said and the abbot gives a blessing. When all are seated on the benches, the brothers in turn read three selections from the book on the lectern. After each reading a responsory is sung. [6]"Glory be to the Father" is not sung after the first two responsories, but only after the third reading. [7]As soon as the cantor begins to sing "Glory be to the Father," let all the monks rise from their seats in honor and reverence for the Holy Trinity. [8]Besides the inspired books of the Old and New Testaments, the works read at Vigils should include explanations of Scripture by reputable and orthodox catholic Fathers.

[9]When these three readings and their responsories have been finished, the remaining six

psalms are sung with an "alleluia" refrain. [10]This ended, there follow a reading from the Apostle recited by heart, a versicle and the litany, that is, "Lord, have mercy." [11]And so Vigils are concluded.

## CHAPTER 10. THE ARRANGEMENT OF THE NIGHT OFFICE IN SUMMER

[1]From Easter until the first of November, the winter arrangement for the number of psalms is followed. [2]But because summer nights are shorter, the readings from the book are omitted. In place of the three readings, one from the Old Testament is substituted. This is to be recited by heart, followed by a short responsory. [3]In everything else, the winter arrangement for Vigils is kept. Thus, winter and summer, there are never fewer than twelve psalms at Vigils, not counting Psalms 3 and 94.

## CHAPTER 11. THE CELEBRATION OF VIGILS ON SUNDAY

[1]On Sunday the monks should arise earlier for Vigils. [2]In these Vigils, too, there must be moderation in quantity: first, as we have already indicated, six psalms are said, followed by a versicle. Then the monks, seated on the benches and arranged in their proper order, listen to four readings from the book. After each reading a re-

sponsory is sung, [3]but "Glory be to the Father" is added only to the fourth. When the cantor begins it, all immediately rise in reverence.

[4]After these readings the same order is repeated: six more psalms with refrain as before, a versicle, [5]then four more readings and their responsories, as above. [6]Next, three canticles from the Prophets, chosen by the abbot, are said with an "alleluia" refrain. [7]After a versicle and the abbot's blessing, four New Testament readings follow with their responsories, as above. [8]After the fourth responsory, the abbot begins the hymn "We praise you, God." [9]When that is finished, he reads from the Gospels while all the monks stand with respect and awe. [10]At the conclusion of the Gospel reading, all reply "Amen," and immediately the abbot intones the hymn "To you be praise." After a final blessing, Lauds begin.

[11]This arrangement for Sunday Vigils should be followed at all times, summer and winter, [12]unless—God forbid—the monks happen to arise too late. In that case, the readings or responsories will have to be shortened. [13]Let special care be taken that this not happen, but if it does, the monk at fault is to make due satisfaction to God in the oratory.

CHAPTER 12. THE CELEBRATION OF THE SOLEMNITY OF LAUDS

[1]Sunday Lauds begin with Psalm 66, said straight through without a refrain. [2]Then Psalm

50 follows with an "alleluia" refrain. [3]Lauds continue with Psalms 117 and 62, [4]the Canticle of the Three Young Men, Psalms 148 through 150, a reading from the Apocalypse recited by heart and followed by a responsory, an Ambrosian hymn, a versicle, the Gospel Canticle, the litany and the conclusion.

### CHAPTER 13. THE CELEBRATION OF LAUDS
### ON ORDINARY DAYS

[1]On ordinary weekdays, Lauds are celebrated as follows: [2]First, Psalm 66 is said without a refrain and slightly protracted as on Sunday so that everyone can be present for Psalm 50, which has a refrain. [3]Next, according to custom, two more psalms are said in the following order: [4]on Monday, Psalms 5 and 35; [5]on Tuesday, Psalms 42 and 56; [6]on Wednesday, Psalms 63 and 64; [7]on Thursday, Psalms 87 and 89; [8]on Friday, Psalms 75 and 91; [9]on Saturday, Psalm 142 and the Canticle from Deuteronomy, divided into two sections, with "Glory be to the Father" after each section. [10]On other days, however, a Canticle from the Prophets is said, according to the practice of the Roman Church. [11]Next follow Psalms 148 through 150, a reading from the Apostle recited by heart, a responsory, an Ambrosian hymn, a versicle, the Gospel Canticle, the litany and the conclusion.

[12]Assuredly, the celebration of Lauds and Vespers must never pass by without the superior's

reciting the entire Lord's Prayer at the end for all
to hear, because thorns of contention are likely to
spring up. [13]Thus warned by the pledge they
make to one another in the very words of this
prayer: *Forgive us as we forgive* (Matt 6:12), they
may cleanse themselves of this kind of vice. [14]At
other celebrations, only the final part of the
Lord's Prayer is said aloud, that all may reply:
*But deliver us from evil* (Matt 6:13).

### CHAPTER 14. THE CELEBRATION OF VIGILS ON THE ANNIVERSARIES OF SAINTS

[1]On the feasts of saints, and indeed on all solemn festivals, the Sunday order of celebration is
followed, [2]although the psalms, refrains and
readings proper to the day itself are said. The
procedure, however, remains the same as indicated above.

### CHAPTER 15. THE TIMES FOR SAYING ALLELUIA

[1]From the holy feast of Easter until Pentecost,
"alleluia" is always said with both the psalms
and the responsories. [2]Every night from Pentecost until the beginning of Lent, it is said only
with the last six psalms of Vigils. [3]Vigils, Lauds,
Prime, Terce, Sext and None are said with "alleluia" every Sunday except in Lent; at Vespers,
however, a refrain is used. [4]"Alleluia" is never
said with responsories except from Easter to
Pentecost.

CHAPTER 16. THE CELEBRATION OF THE
DIVINE OFFICE DURING THE DAY

[1]The Prophet says: *Seven times a day have I praised you* (Ps 118[119]:164). [2]We will fulfill this sacred number of seven if we satisfy our obligations of service at Lauds, Prime, Terce, Sext, None, Vespers and Compline, [3]for it was of these hours during the day that he said: *Seven times a day have I praised you* (Ps 118[119]:164). [4]Concerning Vigils, the same Prophet says: *At midnight I arose to give you praise* (Ps 118[119]:62). [5]Therefore, we should *praise* our Creator *for his just judgments* at these times: Lauds, Prime, Terce, Sext, None, Vespers and Compline; and *let us arise at night to give* him *praise* (Ps 118[119]:164,62).

CHAPTER 17. THE NUMBER OF PSALMS TO BE SUNG
AT THESE HOURS

[1]We have already established the order for psalmody at Vigils and Lauds. Now let us arrange the remaining hours.

[2]Three psalms are to be said at Prime, each followed by "Glory be to the Father." [3]The hymn for this hour is sung after the opening versicle, *God, come to my assistance* (Ps 69[70]:2), before the psalmody begins. [4]One reading follows the three psalms, and the hour is concluded with a versicle, "Lord, have mercy" and the dismissal.

[5]Prayer is celebrated in the same way at Terce, Sext and None: that is, the opening verse, the

hymn appropriate to each hour, three psalms, a reading with a versicle, "Lord, have mercy" and the dismissal. [6]If the community is rather large, refrains are used with the psalms; if it is smaller, the psalms are said without refrain.

[7]At Vespers the number of psalms should be limited to four, with refrain. [8]After these psalms there follow: a reading and responsory, an Ambrosian hymn, a versicle, the Gospel Canticle, the litany, and, immediately before the dismissal, the Lord's Prayer.

[9]Compline is limited to three psalms without refrain. [10]After the psalmody comes the hymn for this hour, followed by a reading, a versicle, "Lord, have mercy," a blessing and the dismissal.

## CHAPTER 18. THE ORDER OF THE PSALMODY

[1]Each of the day hours begins with the verse, *God, come to my assistance; Lord, make haste to help me* (Ps 69[70]:2), followed by "Glory be to the Father" and the appropriate hymn.

[2]Then, on Sunday at Prime, four sections of Psalm 118 are said. [3]At the other hours, that is, at Terce, Sext and None, three sections of this psalm are said. [4]On Monday three psalms are said at Prime: Psalms 1, 2 and 6. [5]At Prime each day thereafter until Sunday, three psalms are said in consecutive order as far as Psalm 19. Psalms 9 and 17 are each divided into two sections. [6]In this way, Sunday Vigils can always begin with Psalm 20.

⁷On Monday at Terce, Sext and None, the remaining nine sections of Psalm 118 are said, three sections at each hour. ⁸Psalm 118 is thus completed in two days, Sunday and Monday. ⁹On Tuesday, three psalms are said at each of the hours of Terce, Sext and None. These are the nine psalms, 119 through 127. ¹⁰The same psalms are repeated at these hours daily up to Sunday. Likewise, the arrangement of hymns, readings and versicles for these days remains the same. ¹¹In this way, Psalm 118 will always begin on Sunday.

¹²Four psalms are sung each day at Vespers, ¹³starting with Psalm 109 and ending with Psalm 147, ¹⁴omitting the psalms in this series already assigned to other hours, namely, Psalms 117 through 127, Psalm 133 and Psalm 142. ¹⁵All the remaining psalms are said at Vespers. ¹⁶Since this leaves three psalms too few, the longer ones in the series should be divided: that is, Psalms 138, 143 and 144. ¹⁷And because Psalm 116 is short, it can be joined to Psalm 115. ¹⁸This is the order of psalms for Vespers; the rest is as arranged above: the reading, responsory, hymn, versicle and canticle.

¹⁹The same psalms—4, 90 and 133—are said each day at Compline.

²⁰The remaining psalms not accounted for in this arrangement for the day hours are distributed evenly at Vigils over the seven nights of the week. ²¹Longer psalms are to be divided so that twelve psalms are said each night.

²²Above all else we urge that if anyone finds this distribution of the psalms unsatisfactory, he should arrange whatever he judges better, ²³provided that the full complement of one hundred and fifty psalms is by all means carefully maintained every week, and that the series begins anew each Sunday at Vigils. ²⁴For monks who in a week's time say less than the full psalter with the customary canticles betray extreme indolence and lack of devotion in their service. ²⁵We read, after all, that our holy Fathers, energetic as they were, did all this in a single day. Let us hope that we, lukewarm as we are, can achieve it in a whole week.

CHAPTER 19. THE DISCIPLINE OF PSALMODY

¹We believe that the divine presence is everywhere and *that in every place the eyes of the Lord are watching the good and the wicked* (Prov 15:3). ²But beyond the least doubt we should believe this to be especially true when we celebrate the divine office.

³We must always remember, therefore, what the Prophet says: *Serve the Lord with fear* (Ps 2:11), ⁴and again, *Sing praise wisely* (Ps 46[47]:8); ⁵and, *In the presence of the angels I will sing to you* (Ps 137[138]:1). ⁶Let us consider, then, how we ought to behave in the presence of God and his angels, ⁷and let us stand to sing the psalms in such a way that our minds are in harmony with our voices.

## CHAPTER 20. REVERENCE IN PRAYER

¹Whenever we want to ask some favor of a powerful man, we do it humbly and respectfully, for fear of presumption. ²How much more important, then, to lay our petitions before the Lord God of all things with the utmost humility and sincere devotion. ³We must know that God regards our purity of heart and tears of compunction, not our many words. ⁴Prayer should therefore be short and pure, unless perhaps it is prolonged under the inspiration of divine grace. ⁵In community, however, prayer should always be brief; and when the superior gives the signal, all should rise together.

## CHAPTER 21. THE DEANS OF THE MONASTERY

¹If the community is rather large, some brothers chosen for their good repute and holy life should be made deans. ²They will take care of their groups of ten, managing all affairs according to the commandments of God and the orders of their abbot. ³The deans selected should be the kind of men with whom the abbot can confidently share the burdens of his office. ⁴They are to be chosen for virtuous living and wise teaching, not for their rank.

⁵If perhaps one of these deans is found to be puffed up with any pride, and so deserving of censure, he is to be reproved once, twice and even a third time. Should he refuse to amend, he

must be removed from office ⁶and replaced by another who is worthy. ⁷We prescribe the same course of action in regard to the prior.

## CHAPTER 22. THE SLEEPING ARRANGEMENTS OF THE MONKS

¹The monks are to sleep in separate beds. ²They receive bedding as provided by the abbot, suitable to monastic life.

³If possible, all are to sleep in one place, but should the size of the community preclude this, they will sleep in groups of ten or twenty under the watchful care of seniors. ⁴A lamp must be kept burning in the room until morning.

⁵They sleep clothed, and girded with belts or cords; but they should remove their knives, lest they accidentally cut themselves in their sleep. ⁶Thus the monks will always be ready to arise without delay when the signal is given; each will hasten to arrive at the Work of God before the others, yet with all dignity and decorum. ⁷The younger brothers should not have their beds next to each other, but interspersed among those of the seniors. ⁸On arising for the Work of God, they will quietly encourage each other, for the sleepy like to make excuses.

## CHAPTER 23. EXCOMMUNICATION FOR FAULTS

¹If a brother is found to be stubborn or disobedient or proud, if he grumbles or in any way de-

spises the holy rule and defies the orders of his seniors, [2]he should be warned twice privately by the seniors in accord with our Lord's injunction (Matt 18:15-16). [3]If he does not amend, he must be rebuked publicly in the presence of everyone. [4]But if even then he does not reform, let him be excommunicated, provided that he understands the nature of this punishment. [5]If however he lacks understanding, let him undergo corporal punishment.

CHAPTER 24. DEGREES OF EXCOMMUNICATION

[1]There ought to be due proportion between the seriousness of a fault and the measure of excommunication or discipline. [2]The abbot determines the gravity of faults.

[3]If a brother is found guilty of less serious faults, he will not be allowed to share the common table. [4]Anyone excluded from the common table will conduct himself as follows: in the oratory he will not lead a psalm or a refrain nor will he recite a reading until he has made satisfaction, [5]and he will take his meals alone, after the brothers have eaten. [6]For instance, if the brothers eat at noon, he will eat in midafternoon; if the brothers eat in midafternoon, he will eat in the evening, [7]until by proper satisfaction he gains pardon.

CHAPTER 25.  SERIOUS FAULTS

¹A brother guilty of a serious fault is to be excluded from both the table and the oratory. ²No other brother should associate or converse with him at all. ³He will work alone at the tasks assigned to him, living continually in sorrow and penance, pondering that fearful judgment of the Apostle: ⁴*Such a man is handed over for the destruction of his flesh that his spirit may be saved on the day of the Lord* (1 Cor 5:5). ⁵Let him take his food alone in an amount and at a time the abbot considers appropriate for him. ⁶He should not be blessed by anyone passing by, nor should the food that is given him be blessed.

CHAPTER 26.  UNAUTHORIZED ASSOCIATION WITH
THE EXCOMMUNICATED

¹If a brother, acting without an order from the abbot, presumes to associate in any way with an excommunicated brother, to converse with him or to send him a message, ²he should receive a like punishment of excommunication.

CHAPTER 27.  THE ABBOT'S CONCERN FOR THE
EXCOMMUNICATED

¹The abbot must exercise the utmost care and concern for wayward brothers, because *it is not the healthy who need a physician, but the sick*

(Matt 9:12). ²Therefore, he ought to use every skill of a wise physician and send in *senpectae*, that is, mature and wise brothers ³who, under the cloak of secrecy, may support the wavering brother, urge him to be humble as a way of making satisfaction, and *console* him *lest he be overwhelmed by excessive sorrow* (2 Cor 2:7). ⁴Rather, as the Apostle also says: *Let love for him be reaffirmed* (2 Cor 2:8), and let all pray for him.

⁵It is the abbot's responsibility to have great concern and to act with all speed, discernment and diligence in order not to lose any of the sheep entrusted to him. ⁶He should realize that he has undertaken care of the sick, not tyranny over the healthy. ⁷Let him also fear the threat of the Prophet in which God says: *What you saw to be fat you claimed for yourselves, and what was weak you cast aside* (Ezek 34:3-4). ⁸He is to imitate the loving example of the Good Shepherd who left the ninety-nine sheep in the mountains and went in search of the one sheep that had strayed. ⁹So great was his compassion for its weakness that *he* mercifully *placed it on his* sacred *shoulders* and so carried it back to the flock (Luke 15:5).

## CHAPTER 28. THOSE WHO REFUSE TO AMEND AFTER FREQUENT REPROOFS

¹If a brother has been reproved frequently for any fault, or if he has even been excommunicated, yet does not amend, let him receive a

sharper punishment: that is, let him feel the strokes of the rod. ²But if even then he does not reform, or perhaps becomes proud and would actually defend his conduct, which God forbid, the abbot should follow the procedure of a wise physician. ³After he has applied compresses, the ointment of encouragement, the medicine of divine Scripture, and finally the cauterizing iron of excommunication and strokes of the rod, ⁴and if he then perceives that his earnest efforts are unavailing, let him apply an even better remedy: he and all the brothers should pray for him ⁵so that the Lord, who can do all things, may bring about the health of the sick brother. ⁶Yet if even this procedure does not heal him, then finally, the abbot must use the knife and amputate. For the Apostle says: *Banish the evil one from your midst* (1 Cor 5:13); ⁷and again, *If the unbeliever departs, let him depart* (1 Cor 7:15), ⁸lest one diseased sheep infect the whole flock.

### CHAPTER 29. READMISSION OF BROTHERS WHO LEAVE THE MONASTERY

¹If a brother, following his own evil ways, leaves the monastery but then wishes to return, he must first promise to make full amends for leaving. ²Let him be received back, but as a test of his humility he should be given the last place. ³If he leaves again, or even a third time, he should be readmitted under the same conditions. After this, however, he must understand that he will be denied all prospect of return.

CHAPTER 30. THE MANNER OF REPROVING BOYS

¹Every age and level of understanding should receive appropriate treatment. ²Therefore, as often as boys and the young, or those who cannot understand the seriousness of the penalty of excommunication, ³are guilty of misdeeds, they should be subjected to severe fasts or checked with sharp strokes so that they may be healed.

CHAPTER 31. QUALIFICATIONS OF THE MONASTERY CELLARER

¹As cellarer of the monastery, there should be chosen from the community someone who is wise, mature in conduct, temperate, not an excessive eater, not proud, excitable, offensive, dilatory or wasteful, ²but God-fearing, and like a father to the whole community. ³He will take care of everything, ⁴but will do nothing without an order from the abbot. ⁵Let him keep to his orders.

⁶He should not annoy the brothers. ⁷If any brother happens to make an unreasonable demand of him, he should not reject him with disdain and cause him distress, but reasonably and humbly deny the improper request. ⁸Let him keep watch over his own soul, ever mindful of that saying of the Apostle: *He who serves well secures a good standing for himself* (1 Tim 3:13). ⁹He must show every care and concern for the sick, children, guests and the poor, knowing for certain that he will be held accountable for all of

them on the day of judgment. ¹⁰He will regard all utensils and goods of the monastery as sacred vessels of the altar, ¹¹aware that nothing is to be neglected. ¹²He should not be prone to greed, nor be wasteful and extravagant with the goods of the monastery, but should do everything with moderation and according to the abbot's orders.

¹³Above all, let him be humble. If goods are not available to meet a request, he will offer a kind word in reply, ¹⁴for it is written: A kind *word is better than the best gift* (Sir 18:17). ¹⁵He should take care of all that the abbot entrusts to him, and not presume to do what the abbot has forbidden. ¹⁶He will provide the brothers their allotted amount of food without any pride or delay, lest they be led astray. For he must remember what the Scripture says that person deserves *who leads one of the little ones astray* (Matt 18:6).

¹⁷If the community is rather large, he should be given helpers, that with their assistance he may calmly perform the duties of his office. ¹⁸Necessary items are to be requested and given at the proper times, ¹⁹so that no one may be disquieted or distressed in the house of God.

CHAPTER 32. THE TOOLS AND GOODS OF THE MONASTERY

¹The goods of the monastery, that is, its tools, clothing or anything else, should be entrusted to brothers whom the abbot appoints and in whose manner of life he has confidence. ²He will, as he

sees fit, issue to them the various articles to be cared for and collected after use. ³The abbot will maintain a list of these, so that when the brothers succeed one another in their assigned tasks, he may be aware of what he hands out and what he receives back.

⁴Whoever fails to keep the things belonging to the monastery clean or treats them carelessly should be reproved. ⁵If he does not amend, let him be subjected to the discipline of the rule.

## CHAPTER 33. MONKS AND PRIVATE OWNERSHIP

¹Above all, this evil practice must be uprooted and removed from the monastery. ²We mean that without an order from the abbot, no one may presume to give, receive ³or retain anything as his own, nothing at all — not a book, writing tablets or stylus — in short, not a single item, ⁴especially since monks may not have the free disposal even of their own bodies and wills. ⁵For their needs, they are to look to the father of the monastery, and are not allowed anything which the abbot has not given or permitted. ⁶*All things should be the common possession* of all, as it is written, *so that no one* presumes to *call anything his own* (Acts 4:32).

⁷But if anyone is caught indulging in this most evil practice, he should be warned a first and a second time. ⁸If he does not amend, let him be subjected to punishment.

## CHAPTER 34. DISTRIBUTION OF GOODS
### ACCORDING TO NEED

[1]It is written: *Distribution was made to each one as he had need* (Acts 4:35). [2]By this we do not imply that there should be favoritism—God forbid—but rather consideration for weaknesses. [3]Whoever needs less should thank God and not be distressed, [4]but whoever needs more should feel humble because of his weakness, not self-important because of the kindness shown him. [5]In this way all the members will be at peace. [6]First and foremost, there must be no word or sign of the evil of grumbling, no manifestation of it for any reason at all. [7]If, however, anyone is caught grumbling, let him undergo more severe discipline.

## CHAPTER 35. KITCHEN SERVERS OF THE WEEK

[1]The brothers should serve one another. Consequently, no one will be excused from kitchen service unless he is sick or engaged in some important business of the monastery, [2]for such service increases reward and fosters love. [3]Let those who are not strong have help so that they may serve without distress, [4]and let everyone receive help as the size of the community or local conditions warrant. [5]If the community is rather large, the cellarer should be excused from kitchen service, and, as we have said, those should also be excused who are engaged in important business. [6]Let all the rest serve one another in love.

⁷On Saturday the brother who is completing his work will do the washing. ⁸He is to wash the towels which the brothers use to wipe their hands and feet. ⁹Both the one who is ending his service and the one who is about to begin are to wash the feet of everyone. ¹⁰The utensils required for the kitchen service are to be washed and returned intact to the cellarer, ¹¹who in turn issues them to the one beginning his week. In this way the cellarer will know what he hands out and what he receives back.

¹²An hour before mealtime, the kitchen workers of the week should each receive a drink and some bread over and above the regular portion, ¹³so that at mealtime, they may serve their brothers without grumbling or hardship. ¹⁴On solemn days, however, they should wait until after the dismissal.

¹⁵On Sunday immediately after Lauds, those beginning as well as those completing their week of service should make a profound bow in the oratory before all and ask for their prayers. ¹⁶Let the server completing his week recite this verse: *Blessed are you, Lord God*, who *have helped me and comforted me* (Dan 3:52; Ps 85[86]:17). ¹⁷After this verse has been said three times, he receives a blessing. Then the one beginning his service follows and says: *God, come to my assistance; Lord, make haste to help me* (Ps 69[70]:2). ¹⁸And all repeat this verse three times. When he has received a blessing, he begins his service.

CHAPTER 36. THE SICK BROTHERS

[1]Care of the sick must rank above and before all else, so that they may truly be served as Christ, [2]for he said: *I was sick and you visited me* (Matt 25:36), [3]and, *What you did for one of these least brothers you did for me* (Matt 25:40). [4]Let the sick on their part bear in mind that they are served out of honor for God, and let them not by their excessive demands distress their brothers who serve them. [5]Still, sick brothers must be patiently borne with, because serving them leads to a greater reward. [6]Consequently, the abbot should be extremely careful that they suffer no neglect.

[7]Let a separate room be designated for the sick, and let them be served by an attendant who is God-fearing, attentive and concerned. [8]The sick may take baths whenever it is advisable, but the healthy, and especially the young, should receive permission less readily. [9]Moreover, to regain their strength, the sick who are very weak may eat meat, but when their health improves, they should all abstain from meat as usual.

[10]The abbot must take the greatest care that cellarers and those who serve the sick do not neglect them, for the shortcomings of disciples are his responsibility.

CHAPTER 37. THE ELDERLY AND CHILDREN

[1]Although human nature itself is inclined to be compassionate toward the old and the young, the

authority of the rule should also provide for them.
²Since their lack of strength must always be taken
into account, they should certainly not be required to follow the strictness of the rule with
regard to food, ³but should be treated with kindly
consideration and allowed to eat before the regular hours.

CHAPTER 38. THE READER FOR THE WEEK

¹Reading will always accompany the meals of
the brothers. The reader should not be the one
who just happens to pick up the book, but someone who will read for a whole week, beginning
on Sunday. ²After Mass and Communion, let the
incoming reader ask all to pray for him so that
God may shield him from the spirit of vanity.
³Let him begin this verse in the oratory: *Lord,
open my lips, and my mouth shall proclaim your
praise* (Ps 50[51]:17), and let all say it three
times. ⁴When he has received a blessing, he will
begin his week of reading.

⁵Let there be complete silence. No whisper-
ing, no speaking — only the reader's voice should
be heard there. ⁶The brothers should by turn
serve one another's needs as they eat and drink,
so that no one need ask for anything. ⁷If, however, anything is required, it should be requested
by an audible signal of some kind rather than by
speech. ⁸No one should presume to ask a question about the reading or about anything else, *lest*

*occasion be given* [to the devil] (Eph 4:27; 1 Tim 5:14). ⁹The superior, however, may wish to say a few words of instruction.

¹⁰Because of holy Communion and because the fast may be too hard for him to bear, the brother who is reader for the week is to receive some diluted wine before he begins to read. ¹¹Afterward he will take his meal with the weekly kitchen servers and the attendants.

¹²Brothers will read and sing, not according to rank, but according to their ability to benefit their hearers.

### CHAPTER 39. THE PROPER AMOUNT OF FOOD

¹For the daily meals, whether at noon or in midafternoon, it is enough, we believe, to provide all tables with two kinds of cooked food because of individual weaknesses. ²In this way, the person who may not be able to eat one kind of food may partake of the other. ³Two kinds of cooked food, therefore, should suffice for all the brothers, and if fruit or fresh vegetables are available, a third dish may also be added. ⁴A generous pound of bread is enough for a day whether for only one meal or for both dinner and supper. ⁵In the latter case the cellarer will set aside one third of this pound and give it to the brothers at supper.

⁶Should it happen that the work is heavier than usual, the abbot may decide—and he will have the authority—to grant something additional, provided that it is appropriate, ⁷and that above all

overindulgence is avoided, lest a monk experience indigestion. ⁸For nothing is so inconsistent with the life of any Christian as overindulgence. ⁹Our Lord says: *Take care that your hearts are not weighed down with overindulgence* (Luke 21:34).

¹⁰Young boys should not receive the same amount as their elders, but less, since in all matters frugality is the rule. ¹¹Let everyone, except the sick who are very weak, abstain entirely from eating the meat of four-footed animals.

### CHAPTER 40. THE PROPER AMOUNT OF DRINK

¹*Everyone has his own gift from God, one this and another that* (1 Cor 7:7). ²It is, therefore, with some uneasiness that we specify the amount of food and drink for others. ³However, with due regard for the infirmities of the sick, we believe that a half bottle of wine a day is sufficient for each. ⁴But those to whom God gives the strength to abstain must know that they will earn their own reward.

⁵The superior will determine when local conditions, work or the summer heat indicates the need for a greater amount. He must, in any case, take great care lest excess or drunkenness creep in. ⁶We read that monks should not drink wine at all, but since the monks of our day cannot be convinced of this, let us at least agree to drink moderately, and not to the point of excess, ⁷for *wine makes even wise men go astray* (Sir 19:2).

⁸However, where local circumstances dictate an amount much less than what is stipulated above, or even none at all, those who live there should bless God and not grumble. ⁹Above all else we admonish them to refrain from grumbling.

## CHAPTER 41. THE TIMES FOR THE BROTHERS' MEALS

¹From holy Easter to Pentecost, the brothers eat at noon and take supper in the evening. ²Beginning with Pentecost and continuing throughout the summer, the monks fast until midafternoon on Wednesday and Friday, unless they are working in the fields or the summer heat is oppressive.

³On the other days they eat dinner at noon. ⁴Indeed, the abbot may decide that they should continue to eat dinner at noon every day if they have work in the fields or if the summer heat remains extreme. ⁵Similarly, he should so regulate and arrange all matters that souls may be saved and the brothers may go about their activities without justifiable grumbling.

⁶From the thirteenth of September to the beginning of Lent, they always take their meal in midafternoon. ⁷Finally, from the beginning of Lent to Easter, they eat towards evening. ⁸Let Vespers be celebrated early enough so that there is no need for a lamp while eating, and that everything can be finished by daylight. ⁹Indeed, at all times let supper or the hour of the fast-day

meal be so scheduled that everything can be done by daylight.

## CHAPTER 42.  SILENCE AFTER COMPLINE

[1]Monks should diligently cultivate silence at all times, but especially at night. [2]Accordingly, this will always be the arrangement whether for fast days or for ordinary days. [3]When there are two meals, all the monks will sit together immediately after rising from supper. Someone should read from the *Conferences* or the *Lives* of the Fathers or at any rate something else that will benefit the hearers, [4]but not the Heptateuch or the Books of Kings, because it will not be good for those of weak understanding to hear these writings at that hour; they should be read at other times.

[5]On fast days there is to be a short interval between Vespers and the reading of the *Conferences*, as we have indicated. [6]Then let four or five pages be read, or as many as time permits. [7]This reading period will allow for all to come together, in case any were engaged in assigned tasks. [8]When all have assembled, they should pray Compline; and on leaving Compline, no one will be permitted to speak further. [9]If anyone is found to transgress this rule of silence, he must be subjected to severe punishment, [10]except on occasions when guests require attention or the abbot wishes to give someone a command, [11]but even this is to be done with the utmost seriousness and proper restraint.

CHAPTER 43. TARDINESS AT THE WORK OF GOD
OR AT TABLE

¹On hearing the signal for an hour of the divine office, the monk will immediately set aside what he has in hand and go with utmost speed, ²yet with gravity and without giving occasion for frivolity. ³Indeed, nothing is to be preferred to the Work of God.

⁴If at Vigils anyone comes after the "Glory be to the Father" of Psalm 94, which we wish, therefore, to be said quite deliberately and slowly, he is not to stand in his regular place in choir. ⁵He must take the last place of all, or one set apart by the abbot for such offenders, that they may be seen by him and by all, ⁶until they do penance by public satisfaction at the end of the Work of God. ⁷We have decided, therefore, that they ought to stand either in the last place or apart from the others so that the attention they attract will shame them into amending. ⁸Should they remain outside the oratory, there may be those who would return to bed and sleep, or, worse yet, settle down outside and engage in idle talk, thereby *giving occasion to the Evil One* (Eph 4:27; 1 Tim 5:14). ⁹They should come inside so that they will not lose everything and may amend in the future.

¹⁰At the day hours the same rule applies to anyone who comes after the opening verse and the "Glory be to the Father" of the first psalm following it: he is to stand in the last place. ¹¹Until he has made satisfaction, he is not to presume

to join the choir of those praying the psalms, unless perhaps the abbot pardons him and grants an exception. [12]Even in this case, the one at fault is still bound to satisfaction.

[13]But, if anyone does not come to table before the verse so that all may say the verse and pray and sit down at table together, [14]and if this failure happens through the individual's own negligence or fault, he should be reproved up to the second time. [15]If he still does not amend, let him not be permitted to share the common table, [16]but take his meals alone, separated from the company of all. His portion of wine should be taken away until there is satisfaction and amendment. [17]Anyone not present for the verse said after meals is to be treated in the same manner.

[18]No one is to presume to eat or drink before or after the time appointed. [19]Moreover, if anyone is offered something by a superior and refuses it, then, if later he wants what he refused or anything else, he should receive nothing at all until he has made appropriate amends.

CHAPTER 44.  SATISFACTION BY THE
EXCOMMUNICATED

[1]Anyone excommunicated for serious faults from the oratory and from the table is to prostrate himself in silence at the oratory entrance at the end of the celebration of the Work of God. [2]He

should lie face down at the feet of all as they leave the oratory, ³and let him do this until the abbot judges he has made satisfaction. ⁴Next, at the bidding of the abbot, he is to prostrate himself at the abbot's feet, then at the feet of all that they may pray for him. ⁵Only then, if the abbot orders, should he be admitted to the choir in the rank the abbot assigns. ⁶Even so, he should not presume to lead a psalm or a reading or anything else in the oratory without further instructions from the abbot. ⁷In addition, at all the hours, as the Work of God is being completed, he must prostrate himself in the place he occupies. ⁸He will continue this form of satisfaction until the abbot again bids him cease.

⁹Those excommunicated for less serious faults from the table only are to make satisfaction in the oratory for as long as the abbot orders. ¹⁰They do so until he gives his blessing and says: "Enough."

CHAPTER 45. MISTAKES IN THE ORATORY

¹Should anyone make a mistake in a psalm, responsory, refrain or reading, he must make satisfaction there before all. If he does not use this occasion to humble himself, he will be subjected to more severe punishment ²for failing to correct by humility the wrong committed through negligence. ³Children, however, are to be whipped for such a fault.

CHAPTER 46.  FAULTS COMMITTED IN OTHER
MATTERS

¹If someone commits a fault while at any
work—while working in the kitchen, in the
storeroom, in serving, in the bakery, in the garden, in any craft or anywhere else— ²either by
breaking or losing something or failing in any
other way in any other place, ³he must at once
come before the abbot and community and of his
own accord admit his fault and make satisfaction.
⁴If it is made known through another, he is to be
subjected to a more severe correction.

⁵When the cause of the sin lies hidden in his
conscience, he is to reveal it only to the abbot or
to one of the spiritual elders, ⁶who know how to
heal their own wounds as well as those of others,
without exposing them and making them public.

CHAPTER 47.  ANNOUNCING THE HOURS FOR THE
WORK OF GOD

¹It is the abbot's care to announce, day and
night, the hour for the Work of God. He may do so
personally or delegate the responsibility to a con-
scientious brother, so that everything may be
done at the proper time.

²Only those so authorized are to lead psalms
and refrains, after the abbot according to their
rank. ³No one should presume to read or sing
unless he is able to benefit the hearers; ⁴let this
be done with humility, seriousness and reverence, and at the abbot's bidding.

CHAPTER 48. THE DAILY MANUAL LABOR

¹Idleness is the enemy of the soul. Therefore, the brothers should have specified periods for manual labor as well as for prayerful reading.

²We believe that the times for both may be arranged as follows: ³From Easter to the first of October, they will spend their mornings after Prime till about the fourth hour at whatever work needs to be done. ⁴From the fourth hour until the time of Sext, they will devote themselves to reading. ⁵But after Sext and their meal, they may rest on their beds in complete silence; should a brother wish to read privately, let him do so, but without disturbing the others. ⁶They should say None a little early, about midway through the eighth hour, and then until Vespers they are to return to whatever work is necessary. ⁷They must not become distressed if local conditions or their poverty should force them to do the harvesting themselves. ⁸When they live by the labor of their hands, as our fathers and the apostles did, then they are really monks. ⁹Yet, all things are to be done with moderation on account of the fainthearted.

¹⁰From the first of October to the beginning of Lent, the brothers ought to devote themselves to reading until the end of the second hour. ¹¹At this time Terce is said and they are to work at their assigned tasks until None. ¹²At the first signal for the hour of None, all put aside their work to be ready for the second signal. ¹³Then after their

meal they will devote themselves to their reading
or to the psalms.

¹⁴During the days of Lent, they should be
free in the morning to read until the third hour,
after which they will work at their assigned
tasks until the end of the tenth hour. ¹⁵During
this time of Lent each one is to receive a book
from the library, and is to read the whole of it
straight through. ¹⁶These books are to be distributed at the beginning of Lent.

¹⁷Above all, one or two seniors must surely be
deputed to make the rounds of the monastery
while the brothers are reading. ¹⁸Their duty is to
see that no brother is so apathetic as to waste time
or engage in idle talk to the neglect of his reading, and so not only harm himself but also distract
others. ¹⁹If such a monk is found — God forbid —
he should be reproved a first and a second time.
²⁰If he does not amend, he must be subjected to
the punishment of the rule as a warning to others.
²¹Further, brothers ought not to associate with
one another at inappropriate times.

²²On Sunday all are to be engaged in reading
except those who have been assigned various
duties. ²³If anyone is so remiss and indolent that
he is unwilling or unable to study or to read, he is
to be given some work in order that he may not
be idle.

²⁴Brothers who are sick or weak should be
given a type of work or craft that will keep them
busy without overwhelming them or driving
them away. ²⁵The abbot must take their infirmities into account.

CHAPTER 49. THE OBSERVANCE OF LENT

¹The life of a monk ought to be a continuous Lent. ²Since few, however, have the strength for this, we urge the entire community during these days of Lent to keep its manner of life most pure ³and to wash away in this holy season the negligences of other times. ⁴This we can do in a fitting manner by refusing to indulge evil habits and by devoting ourselves to prayer with tears, to reading, to compunction of heart and self-denial. ⁵During these days, therefore, we will add to the usual measure of our service something by way of private prayer and abstinence from food or drink, ⁶so that each of us will have something above the assigned measure to offer God of his own will *with the joy of the Holy Spirit* (1 Thess 1:6). ⁷In other words, let each one deny himself some food, drink, sleep, needless talking and idle jesting, and look forward to holy Easter with joy and spiritual longing.

⁸Everyone should, however, make known to the abbot what he intends to do, since it ought to be done with his prayer and approval. ⁹Whatever is undertaken without the permission of the spiritual father will be reckoned as presumption and vainglory, not deserving a reward. ¹⁰Therefore, everything must be done with the abbot's approval.

### CHAPTER 50. BROTHERS WORKING AT A DISTANCE OR TRAVELING

¹Brothers who work so far away that they cannot return to the oratory at the proper time— ²and the abbot determines that is the case— ³are to perform the Work of God where they are, and kneel out of reverence for God.

⁴So too, those who have been sent on a journey are not to omit the prescribed hours but to observe them as best they can, not neglecting their measure of service.

### CHAPTER 51. BROTHERS ON A SHORT JOURNEY

¹If a brother is sent on some errand and expects to return to the monastery that same day, he must not presume to eat outside, even if he receives a pressing invitation, ²unless perhaps the abbot has ordered it. ³Should he act otherwise, he will be excommunicated.

### CHAPTER 52. THE ORATORY OF THE MONASTERY

¹The oratory ought to be what it is called, and nothing else is to be done or stored there. ²After the Work of God, all should leave in complete silence and with reverence for God, ³so that a brother who may wish to pray alone will not be disturbed by the insensitivity of another. ⁴Moreover, if at other times someone chooses to pray privately, he may simply go in and pray, not

in a loud voice, but with tears and heartfelt devotion. [5]Accordingly, anyone who does not pray in
this manner is not to remain in the oratory after
the Work of God, as we have said; then he will
not interfere with anyone else.

### CHAPTER 53. THE RECEPTION OF GUESTS

[1]All guests who present themselves are to be
welcomed as Christ, for he himself will say: *I was
a stranger and you welcomed me* (Matt 25:35).
[2]Proper honor must be shown *to all, especially to
those who share our faith* (Gal 6:10) and to pil-
grims.

[3]Once a guest has been announced, the
superior and the brothers are to meet him with all
the courtesy of love. [4]First of all, they are to pray
together and thus be united in peace, [5]but prayer
must always precede the kiss of peace because of
the delusions of the devil.

[6]All humility should be shown in addressing a
guest on arrival or departure. [7]By a bow of the
head or by a complete prostration of the body,
Christ is to be adored because he is indeed welcomed in them. [8]After the guests have been received, they should be invited to pray; then the
superior or an appointed brother will sit with
them. [9]The divine law is read to the guest for his
instruction, and after that every kindness is
shown to him. [10]The superior may break his fast
for the sake of a guest, unless it is a day of special
fast which cannot be broken. [11]The brothers,

however, observe the usual fast. <sup>12</sup>The abbot shall pour water on the hands of the guests, <sup>13</sup>and the abbot with the entire community shall wash their feet. <sup>14</sup>After the washing they will recite this verse: *God, we have received your mercy in the midst of your temple* (Ps 47[48]:10).

<sup>15</sup>Great care and concern are to be shown in receiving poor people and pilgrims, because in them more particularly Christ is received; our very awe of the rich guarantees them special respect.

<sup>16</sup>The kitchen for the abbot and guests ought to be separate, so that guests—and monasteries are never without them—need not disturb the brothers when they present themselves at unpredictable hours. <sup>17</sup>Each year, two brothers who can do the work competently are to be assigned to this kitchen. <sup>18</sup>Additional help should be available when needed, so that they can perform this service without grumbling. On the other hand, when the work slackens, they are to go wherever other duties are assigned them. <sup>19</sup>This consideration is not for them alone, but applies to all duties in the monastery; <sup>20</sup>the brothers are to be given help when it is needed, and whenever they are free, they work wherever they are assigned.

<sup>21</sup>The guest quarters are to be entrusted to a God-fearing brother. <sup>22</sup>Adequate bedding should be available there. The house of God should be in the care of wise men who will manage it wisely.

²³No one is to speak or associate with guests unless he is bidden; ²⁴however, if a brother meets or sees a guest, he is to greet him humbly, as we have said. He asks for a blessing and continues on his way, explaining that he is not allowed to speak with a guest.

## CHAPTER 54. LETTERS OR GIFTS FOR MONKS

¹In no circumstances is a monk allowed, unless the abbot says he may, to exchange letters, blessed tokens or small gifts of any kind, with his parents or anyone else, or with a fellow monk. ²He must not presume to accept gifts sent him even by his parents without previously telling the abbot. ³If the abbot orders acceptance, he still has the power to give the gift to whom he will; ⁴and the brother for whom it was originally sent must not be distressed, *lest occasion be given to the devil* (Eph 4:27; 1 Tim 5:14). ⁵Whoever presumes to act otherwise will be subjected to the discipline of the rule.

## CHAPTER 55. THE CLOTHING AND FOOTWEAR OF THE BROTHERS

¹The clothing distributed to the brothers should vary according to local conditions and climate, ²because more is needed in cold regions and less in warmer. ³This is left to the abbot's discretion. ⁴We believe that for each monk a cowl and tunic will suffice in temperate regions; ⁵in

winter a woolen cowl is necessary, in summer a thinner or worn one; ⁶also a scapular for work, and footwear—both sandals and shoes.

⁷Monks must not complain about the color or coarseness of all these articles, but use what is available in the vicinity at a reasonable cost. ⁸However, the abbot ought to be concerned about the measurements of these garments that they not be too short but fitted to the wearers.

⁹Whenever new clothing is received, the old should be returned at once and stored in a wardrobe for the poor. ¹⁰To provide for laundering and night wear, every monk will need two cowls and two tunics, ¹¹but anything more must be taken away as superfluous. ¹²When new articles are received, the worn ones—sandals or anything old—must be returned.

¹³Brothers going on a journey should get underclothing from the wardrobe. On their return they are to wash it and give it back. ¹⁴Their cowls and tunics, too, ought to be somewhat better than those they ordinarily wear. Let them get these from the wardrobe before departing, and on returning put them back.

¹⁵For bedding the monks will need a mat, a woolen blanket and a light covering as well as a pillow.

¹⁶The beds are to be inspected frequently by the abbot, lest private possessions be found there. ¹⁷A monk discovered with anything not given him by the abbot must be subjected to very severe punishment. ¹⁸In order that this vice of

private ownership may be completely uprooted, the abbot is to provide all things necessary: ¹⁹that is, cowl, tunic, sandals, shoes, belt, knife, stylus, needle, handkerchief and writing tablets. In this way every excuse of lacking some necessity will be taken away.

²⁰The abbot, however, must always bear in mind what is said in the Acts of the Apostles: *Distribution was made to each one as he had need* (Acts 4:35). ²¹In this way the abbot will take into account the weaknesses of the needy, not the evil will of the envious; ²²yet in all his judgments he must bear in mind God's retribution.

### CHAPTER 56. THE ABBOT'S TABLE

¹The abbot's table must always be with guests and travelers. ²Whenever there are no guests, it is within his right to invite any of the brothers he wishes. ³However, for the sake of maintaining discipline, one or two seniors must always be left with the brothers.

### CHAPTER 57. THE ARTISANS OF THE MONASTERY

¹If there are artisans in the monastery, they are to practice their craft with all humility, but only with the abbot's permission. ²If one of them becomes puffed up by his skillfulness in his craft, and feels that he is conferring something on the monastery, ³he is to be removed from practicing

his craft and not allowed to resume it unless, after manifesting his humility, he is so ordered by the abbot.

⁴Whenever products of these artisans are sold, those responsible for the sale must not dare to practice any fraud. ⁵Let them always remember Ananias and Sapphira, who incurred bodily death (Acts 5:1-11), ⁶lest they and all who perpetrate fraud in monastery affairs suffer spiritual death.

⁷The evil of avarice must have no part in establishing prices, ⁸which should, therefore, always be a little lower than people outside the monastery are able to set, ⁹*so that in all things God may be glorified* (1 Pet 4:11).

### CHAPTER 58. THE PROCEDURE FOR RECEIVING BROTHERS

¹Do not grant newcomers to the monastic life an easy entry, ²but, as the Apostle says, *Test the spirits to see if they are from God* (1 John 4:1). ³Therefore, if someone comes and keeps knocking at the door, and if at the end of four or five days he has shown himself patient in bearing his harsh treatment and difficulty of entry, and has persisted in his request, ⁴then he should be allowed to enter and stay in the guest quarters for a few days. ⁵After that, he should live in the novitiate, where the novices study, eat and sleep.

⁶A senior chosen for his skill in winning souls should be appointed to look after them with careful attention. ⁷The concern must be whether the

novice truly seeks God and whether he shows eagerness for the Work of God, for obedience and for trials. ⁸The novice should be clearly told all the hardships and difficulties that will lead him to God.

⁹If he promises perseverance in his stability, then after two months have elapsed let this rule be read straight through to him, ¹⁰and let him be told: "This is the law under which you are choosing to serve. If you can keep it, come in. If not, feel free to leave." ¹¹If he still stands firm, he is to be taken back to the novitiate, and again thoroughly tested in patience. ¹²After six months have passed, the rule is to be read to him, so that he may know what he is entering. ¹³If once more he stands firm, let four months go by, and then read this rule to him again. ¹⁴If after due reflection he promises to observe everything and to obey every command given him, let him then be received into the community. ¹⁵But he must be well aware that, as the law of the rule establishes, from this day he is no longer free to leave the monastery, ¹⁶nor to shake from his neck the yoke of the rule which, in the course of so prolonged a period of reflection, he was free either to reject or to accept.

¹⁷When he is to be received, he comes before the whole community in the oratory and promises stability, fidelity to monastic life, and obedience. ¹⁸This is done in the presence of God and his saints to impress on the novice that if he ever acts otherwise, he will surely be condemned by

the one he mocks. [19]He states his promise in a document drawn up in the name of the saints whose relics are there, and of the abbot, who is present. [20]The novice writes out this document himself, or if he is illiterate, then he asks someone else to write it for him, but himself puts his mark to it and with his own hand lays it on the altar. [21]After he has put it there, the novice himself begins the verse: *Receive me*, Lord, *as you have promised, and I shall live; do not disappoint me in my hope* (Ps 118[119]:116). [22]The whole community repeats the verse three times, and adds "Glory be to the Father." [23]Then the novice prostrates himself at the feet of each monk to ask his prayers, and from that very day he is to be counted as one of the community.

[24]If he has any possessions, he should either give them to the poor beforehand, or make a formal donation of them to the monastery, without keeping back a single thing for himself, [25]well aware that from that day he will not have even his own body at his disposal. [26]Then and there in the oratory, he is to be stripped of everything of his own that he is wearing and clothed in what belongs to the monastery. [27]The clothing taken from him is to be put away and kept safely in the wardrobe, [28]so that, should he ever agree to the devil's suggestion and leave the monastery—which God forbid—he can be stripped of the clothing of the monastery before he is cast out. [29]But that document of his which the abbot took from the altar should not be given back to him but kept in the monastery.

## CHAPTER 59. THE OFFERING OF SONS BY NOBLES
### OR BY THE POOR

[1]If a member of the nobility offers his son to God in the monastery, and the boy himself is too young, the parents draw up the document mentioned above; [2]then, at the presentation of the gifts, they wrap the document itself and the boy's hand in the altar cloth. That is how they offer him.

[3]As to their property, they either make a sworn promise in this document that they will never personally, never through an intermediary, nor in any way at all, nor at any time, give the boy anything or afford him the opportunity to possess anything; [4]or else, if they are unwilling to do this and still wish to win their reward for making an offering to the monastery, [5]they make a formal donation of the property that they want to give to the monastery, keeping the revenue for themselves, should they so desire. [6]This ought to leave no way open for the boy to entertain any expectations that could deceive and ruin him. May God forbid this, but we have learned from experience that it can happen.

[7]Poor people do the same, [8]but those who have nothing at all simply write the document and, in the presence of witnesses, offer their son with the gifts.

CHAPTER 60. THE ADMISSION OF PRIESTS TO THE
MONASTERY

[1]If any ordained priest asks to be received into
the monastery, do not agree too quickly. [2]However, if he is fully persistent in his request, he
must recognize that he will have to observe the
full discipline of the rule [3]without any mitigation, knowing that it is written: *Friend, what
have you come for* (Matt 26:50)? [4]He should,
however, be allowed to stand next to the abbot, to
give blessings and to celebrate Mass, provided
that the abbot bids him. [5]Otherwise, he must recognize that he is subject to the discipline of the
rule, and not make any exceptions for himself,
but rather give everyone an example of humility.
[6]Whenever there is question of an appointment
or of any other business in the monastery, [7]he
takes the place that corresponds to the date of his
entry into the community, and not that granted
him out of respect for his priesthood.

[8]Any clerics who similarly wish to join the
community should be ranked somewhere in the
middle, [9]but only if they, too, promise to keep the
rule and observe stability.

CHAPTER 61. THE RECEPTION OF VISITING MONKS

[1]A visiting monk from far away will perhaps
present himself and wish to stay as a guest in the
monastery. [2]Provided that he is content with the
life as he finds it, and does not make excessive

demands that upset the monastery, ³but is simply content with what he finds, he should be received for as long a time as he wishes. ⁴He may, indeed, with all humility and love make some reasonable criticisms or observations, which the abbot should prudently consider; it is possible that the Lord guided him to the monastery for this very purpose.

⁵If after a while he wishes to remain and bind himself to stability, he should not be refused this wish, especially as there was time enough, while he was a guest, to judge his character. ⁶But if during his stay he has been found excessive in his demands or full of faults, he should certainly not be admitted as a member of the community. ⁷Instead, he should be politely told to depart, lest his wretched ways contaminate others.

⁸If, however, he has shown that he is not the kind of man who deserves to be dismissed, let him, on his request, be received as a member of the community. ⁹He should even be urged to stay, so that others may learn from his example, ¹⁰because wherever we may be, we are in the service of the same Lord and doing battle for the same King. ¹¹Further, the abbot may set such a man in a somewhat higher place in the community, if he sees that he deserves it. ¹²In fact, whether it is a monk or someone in the priestly or clerical orders mentioned above, the abbot has the power to set any of them above the place that corresponds to the date of his entry, if he sees that his life warrants it.

¹³The abbot must, however, take care never to receive into the community a monk from another known monastery, unless the monk's abbot consents and sends a letter of recommendation, ¹⁴since it is written: *Never do to another what you do not want done to yourself* (Tob 4:16).

## CHAPTER 62. THE PRIESTS OF THE MONASTERY

¹Any abbot who asks to have a priest or deacon ordained should choose from his monks one worthy to exercise the priesthood. ²The monk so ordained must be on guard against conceit or pride, ³must not presume to do anything except what the abbot commands him, and must recognize that now he will have to subject himself all the more to the discipline of the rule. ⁴Just because he is a priest, he may not therefore forget the obedience and discipline of the rule, but must make more and more progress toward God.

⁵He will always take the place that corresponds to the date of his entry into the monastery, ⁶except in his duties at the altar, or unless the whole community chooses and the abbot wishes to give him a higher place for the goodness of his life. ⁷Yet, he must know how to keep the rule established for deans and priors; ⁸should he presume to act otherwise, he must be regarded as a rebel, not as a priest. ⁹If after many warnings he does not improve, let the bishop too be brought in as a witness. ¹⁰Should he not amend even then, and his faults become notorious, he is to be dismissed

from the monastery, [11]but only if he is so arrogant
that he will not submit or obey the rule.

### CHAPTER 63. COMMUNITY RANK

[1]The monks keep their rank in the monastery
according to the date of their entry, the virtue of
their lives, and the decision of the abbot. [2]The
abbot is not to disturb the flock entrusted to him
nor make any unjust arrangements, as though he
had the power to do whatever he wished. [3]He
must constantly reflect that he will have to give
God an account of all his decisions and actions.
[4]Therefore, when the monks come for the kiss of
peace and for Communion, when they lead
psalms or stand in choir, they do so in the order
decided by the abbot or already existing among
them. [5]Absolutely nowhere shall age automati-
cally determine rank. [6]Remember that Samuel
and Daniel were still boys when they judged
their elders (1 Sam 3; Dan 13:44-62). [7]Therefore,
apart from those mentioned above whom the
abbot has for some overriding consideration
promoted, or for a specific reason demoted, all
the rest should keep to the order of their entry.
[8]For example, someone who came to the monastery at the second hour of the day must recognize
that he is junior to someone who came at the first
hour, regardless of age or distinction. [9]Boys,
however, are to be disciplined in everything by
everyone.

[10]The younger monks, then, must respect their

seniors, and the seniors must love their juniors.
11When they address one another, no one should
be allowed to do so simply by name; 12rather, the
seniors call the younger monks "brother" and the
younger monks call their seniors *nonnus*, which
is translated as "venerable father." 13But the abbot, because we believe that he holds the place of
Christ, is to be called "lord" and "abbot," not for
any claim of his own, but out of honor and love
for Christ. 14He, for his part, must reflect on this,
and in his behavior show himself worthy of such
honor.

15Wherever brothers meet, the junior asks his
senior for a blessing. 16When an older monk
comes by, the younger rises and offers him a seat,
and does not presume to sit down unless the
older bids him. 17In this way, they do what the
words of Scripture say: *They should each try to
be the first to show respect to the other* (Rom
12:10).

18In the oratory and at table, small boys and
youths are kept in rank and under discipline.
19Outside or anywhere else, they should be
supervised and controlled until they are old
enough to be responsible.

### CHAPTER 64. THE ELECTION OF AN ABBOT

1In choosing an abbot, the guiding principle
should always be that the man placed in office be
the one selected either by the whole community
acting unanimously in the fear of God, or by some

part of the community, no matter how small, which possesses sounder judgment. ²Goodness of life and wisdom in teaching must be the criteria for choosing the one to be made abbot, even if he is the last in community rank.

³May God forbid that a whole community should conspire to elect a man who goes along with its own evil ways. But if it does, ⁴and if the bishop of the diocese or the abbots or Christians in the area come to know of these evil ways to any extent, ⁵they must block the success of this wicked conspiracy, and set a worthy steward in charge of God's house. ⁶They may be sure that they will receive a generous reward for this, if they do it with pure motives and zeal for God's honor. Conversely, they may be equally sure that to neglect to do so is sinful.

⁷Once in office, the abbot must keep constantly in mind the nature of the burden he has received, and remember to whom he will have *to give an account of his stewardship* (Luke 16:2). ⁸Let him recognize that his goal must be profit for the monks, not preeminence for himself. ⁹He ought, therefore, to be learned in divine law, so that he has a treasury of knowledge from which he can *bring out what is new and what is old* (Matt 13:52). He must be chaste, temperate and merciful. ¹⁰He should always *let mercy triumph over judgment* (Jas 2:13) so that he too may win mercy. ¹¹He must hate faults but love the brothers. ¹²When he must punish them, he should use prudence and avoid extremes; otherwise, by

rubbing too hard to remove the rust, he may break the vessel. ¹³He is to distrust his own frailty and remember *not to crush the bruised reed* (Isa 42:3). ¹⁴By this we do not mean that he should allow faults to flourish, but rather, as we have already said, he should prune them away with prudence and love as he sees best for each individual. ¹⁵Let him strive to be loved rather than feared.

¹⁶Excitable, anxious, extreme, obstinate, jealous or oversuspicious he must not be. Such a man is never at rest. ¹⁷Instead, he must show forethought and consideration in his orders, and whether the task he assigns concerns God or the world, he should be discerning and moderate, ¹⁸bearing in mind the discretion of holy Jacob, who said: *If I drive my flocks too hard, they will all die in a single day* (Gen 33:13). ¹⁹Therefore, drawing on this and other examples of discretion, the mother of virtues, he must so arrange everything that the strong have something to yearn for and the weak nothing to run from.

²⁰He must, above all, keep this rule in every particular, ²¹so that when he has ministered well he will hear from the Lord what that good servant heard who gave his fellow servants grain at the proper time: ²²*I tell you solemnly*, he said, *he sets him over all his possessions* (Matt 24:47).

CHAPTER 65. THE PRIOR OF THE MONASTERY

¹Too often in the past, the appointment of a prior has been the source of serious contention in

monasteries. [2]Some priors, puffed up by the evil spirit of pride and thinking of themselves as second abbots, usurp tyrannical power and foster contention and discord in their communities. [3]This occurs especially in monasteries where the same bishop and the same abbots appoint both abbot and prior. [4]It is easy to see what an absurd arrangement this is, because from the very first moment of his appointment as prior he is given grounds for pride, [5]as his thoughts suggest to him that he is exempt from his abbot's authority. [6]"After all, you were made prior by the same men who made the abbot."

[7]This is an open invitation to envy, quarrels, slander, rivalry, factions and disorders of every kind, [8]with the result that, while abbot and prior pursue conflicting policies, their own souls are inevitably endangered by this discord; [9]and at the same time the monks under them take sides and so go to their ruin. [10]The responsibility for this evil and dangerous situation rests on the heads of those who initiated such a state of confusion.

[11]For the preservation of peace and love we have, therefore, judged it best for the abbot to make all decisions in the conduct of his monastery. [12]If possible, as we have already established, the whole operation of the monastery should be managed through deans under the abbot's direction. [13]Then, so long as it is entrusted to more than one, no individual will yield to

pride. ¹⁴But if local conditions call for it, or the community makes a reasonable and humble request, and the abbot judges it best, ¹⁵then let him, with the advice of God-fearing brothers, choose the man he wants and himself make him his prior. ¹⁶The prior for his part is to carry out respectfully what his abbot assigns to him, and do nothing contrary to the abbot's wishes or arrangements, ¹⁷because the more he is set above the rest, the more he should be concerned to keep what the rule commands.

¹⁸If this prior is found to have serious faults, or is led astray by conceit and grows proud, or shows open contempt for the holy rule, he is to be warned verbally as many as four times. ¹⁹If he does not amend, he is to be punished as required by the discipline of the rule. ²⁰Then, if he still does not reform, he is to be deposed from the rank of prior and replaced by someone worthy. ²¹If after all that, he is not a peaceful and obedient member of the community, he should even be expelled from the monastery. ²²Yet the abbot should reflect that he must give God an account of all his judgments, lest the flames of jealousy or rivalry sear his soul.

### CHAPTER 66. THE PORTER OF THE MONASTERY

¹At the door of the monastery, place a sensible old man who knows how to take a message and deliver a reply, and whose age keeps him from roaming about. ²This porter will need a room

near the entrance so that visitors will always find him there to answer them. ³As soon as anyone knocks, or a poor man calls out, he replies, "Thanks be to God" or "Your blessing, please"; ⁴then, with all the gentleness that comes from the fear of God, he provides a prompt answer with the warmth of love. ⁵Let the porter be given one of the younger brothers if he needs help.

⁶The monastery should, if possible, be so constructed that within it all necessities, such as water, mill and garden are contained, and the various crafts are practiced. ⁷Then there will be no need for the monks to roam outside, because this is not at all good for their souls.

⁸We wish this rule to be read often in the community, so that none of the brothers can offer the excuse of ignorance.

### CHAPTER 67. BROTHERS SENT ON A JOURNEY

¹Brothers sent on a journey will ask the abbot and community to pray for them. ²All absent brothers should always be remembered at the closing prayer of the Work of God. ³When they come back from a journey, they should, on the very day of their return, lie face down on the floor of the oratory at the conclusion of each of the customary hours of the Work of God. ⁴They ask the prayers of all for their faults, in case they may have been caught off guard on the way by seeing some evil thing or hearing some idle talk.

⁵No one should presume to relate to anyone

else what he saw or heard outside the monastery, because that causes the greatest harm. [6]If anyone does so presume, he shall be subjected to the punishment of the rule. [7]So too shall anyone who presumes to leave the enclosure of the monastery, or go anywhere, or do anything at all, however small, without the abbot's order.

## CHAPTER 68. ASSIGNMENT OF IMPOSSIBLE TASKS TO A BROTHER

[1]A brother may be assigned a burdensome task or something he cannot do. If so, he should, with complete gentleness and obedience, accept the order given him. [2]Should he see, however, that the weight of the burden is altogether too much for his strength, then he should choose the appropriate moment and explain patiently to his superior the reasons why he cannot perform the task. [3]This he ought to do without pride, obstinacy or refusal. [4]If after the explanation the superior is still determined to hold to his original order, then the junior must recognize that this is best for him. [5]Trusting in God's help, he must in love obey.

## CHAPTER 69. THE PRESUMPTION OF DEFENDING ANOTHER IN THE MONASTERY

[1]Every precaution must be taken that one monk does not presume in any circumstance to defend another in the monastery or to be his

champion, ²even if they are related by the closest ties of blood. ³In no way whatsoever shall the monks presume to do this, because it can be a most serious source and occasion of contention. ⁴Anyone who breaks this rule is to be sharply restrained.

## CHAPTER 70. THE PRESUMPTION OF STRIKING ANOTHER MONK AT WILL

¹In the monastery every occasion for presumption is to be avoided, ²and so we decree that no one has the authority to excommunicate or strike any of his brothers unless he has been given this power by the abbot. ³*Those who sin should be reprimanded in the presence of all, that the rest may fear* (1 Tim 5:20). ⁴Boys up to the age of fifteen should, however, be carefully controlled and supervised by everyone, ⁵provided that this too is done with moderation and common sense.

⁶If a brother, without the abbot's command, assumes any power over those older or, even in regard to boys, flares up and treats them unreasonably, he is to be subjected to the discipline of the rule. ⁷After all, it is written: *Never do to another what you do not want done to yourself* (Tob 4:16).

## CHAPTER 71. MUTUAL OBEDIENCE

¹Obedience is a blessing to be shown by all, not only to the abbot but also to one another as

brothers, [2]since we know that it is by this way of obedience that we go to God. [3]Therefore, although orders of the abbot or of the priors appointed by him take precedence, and no unofficial order may supersede them, [4]in every other instance younger monks should obey their seniors with all love and concern. [5]Anyone found objecting to this should be reproved.

[6]If a monk is reproved in any way by his abbot or by one of his seniors, even for some very small matter, [7]or if he gets the impression that one of his seniors is angry or disturbed with him, however slightly, [8]he must, then and there without delay, cast himself on the ground at the other's feet to make satisfaction, and lie there until the disturbance is calmed by a blessing. [9]Anyone who refuses to do this should be subjected to corporal punishment or, if he is stubborn, should be expelled from the monastery.

### CHAPTER 72. THE GOOD ZEAL OF MONKS

[1]Just as there is a wicked zeal of bitterness which separates from God and leads to hell, [2]so there is a good zeal which separates from evil and leads to God and everlasting life. [3]This, then, is the good zeal which monks must foster with fervent love: [4]*They should each try to be the first to show respect to the other* (Rom 12:10), [5]supporting with the greatest patience one another's weaknesses of body or behavior, [6]and earnestly competing in obedience to one another. [7]No one

is to pursue what he judges better for himself, but instead, what he judges better for someone else. [8]To their fellow monks they show the pure love of brothers; [9]to God, loving fear; [10]to their abbot, unfeigned and humble love. [11]Let them prefer nothing whatever to Christ, [12]and may he bring us all together to everlasting life.

## CHAPTER 73. THIS RULE ONLY A BEGINNING OF PERFECTION

[1]The reason we have written this rule is that, by observing it in monasteries, we can show that we have some degree of virtue and the beginnings of monastic life. [2]But for anyone hastening on to the perfection of monastic life, there are the teachings of the holy Fathers, the observance of which will lead him to the very heights of perfection. [3]What page, what passage of the inspired books of the Old and New Testaments is not the truest of guides for human life? [4]What book of the holy catholic Fathers does not resoundingly summon us along the true way to reach the Creator? [5]Then, besides the *Conferences* of the Fathers, their *Institutes* and their *Lives*, there is also the rule of our holy father Basil. [6]For observant and obedient monks, all these are nothing less than tools for the cultivation of virtues; [7]but as for us, they make us blush for shame at being so slothful, so unobservant, so negligent. [8]Are you hastening toward your heavenly home? Then with Christ's help, keep this little

rule that we have written for beginners. [9]After that, you can set out for the loftier summits of the teaching and virtues we mentioned above, and under God's protection you will reach them. Amen.